Where Did God Hide His Diamonds?

Copyright © 2011 by Marricke Kofi Gane

Where Did God Hide His Diamonds?

By Marricke Kofi Gane

ISBN: 978-1-909326-27-9

All rights reserved solely by the author. The author guarantees all contents are original and do not infringe upon the legal rights of any other person or work. No part of this book may be reproduced in any form without the permission of the author. For permission requests and others, write to the Author at:

author@marrickekofigane.com

Published by MarrickeGanePublishing

Distributed by Amazon

Where Did God Hide His Diamonds?

(Discovering what exactly God has hidden in you, finding it and prospering freely from it)

By Marricke Kofi GANE

Contents

ACKNOWLEDGEMENTS		ix
FOREWORD		xi
1	Go Now! Go Get a Dream	1
2	Look in Your Hand—That's All You Need	23
3	God Was Ready for You a Long Time Ago	49
4	Lord! Where Did You put the Diamonds?	89
5	Even as Your Soul Prospers—Is He Serious?	119
6	5…4…3…2…1…ACTION!	135
AUTHOR'S OTHER WORKS		153
ABOUT THE AUTHOR		157

DEDICATION

To The One True God Who Reveals All Things

ACKNOWLEDGEMENTS

My first acknowledgement is to the Great and Merciful Lord, Hashem, from whom came everything this book was, is and will ever be. The wisdom is yours O God, and so is the life that wrote it and the souls who read it. Is there really anything that is ours?

* * *

To my parents Gershon and Charity and my siblings - Ivy, Lily and Paul. If I had to choose a family to be born into all over again, I would choose you. First you raised a son, then a man – you couldn't have done a more excellent job. Your prayers have kept me. My peace is your peace.

* * *

To my Spiritual Father, Rev. Dr. James Osborn Nanjo; You have believed in me, you have pushed me to find my path. You have blessed me and you have stood in the gates for me. You have been like a candle – consuming yourself to light the way for me. The life you live has taught me more than a million books would.

FOREWORD

God's glory on the earth is seen through mankind's fulfilment of life and destiny. When mankind fulfils his destiny, it is simply the Glory that God deposited in him/her from the Garden of Eden being revealed to the world. It cannot be denied because of its brightness, just like a diamond. Jesus Christ was the revelation of the Glory of God because He identified what His ministry was and then fulfilled it. He excelled at the one thing He was the only one suited for – to save all humankind.

It was the mirror image of God's idea on how He intended us to live on the earth – fully fulfilled in life and in destiny. When you are really ready for the God kind of uncommon glory in every area of life, you ought to find and walk on the path leading to God's expected end for your life where a fulfilled life, abundance and greatness are the key marks of the beneficiaries. It is finding that right path that will make all the difference. God's plan of unlimited fulfilment and greatness in every area of one's life as gleaned from the original city of Eden and from the life of Christ is still possible today for the redeemed of the Lord, but it can only be accessed by following the kingdom principles outlined in this book. This book by Marricke Kofi

GANE explains how fulfilment of destiny, attaining greatness in the earth and the endless blessings of Eden are intertwined and how you can become a partaker. If you apply the destiny principles explained in this manual, it will surely be well with you in all your ways and you will have great success to the glory of God.

The first man Adam, knew and excelled at his God given purpose, and everything worked in his favour until he fell.

Marricke Kofi GANE, in this book has carefully provided us with exceptional insight on kingdom approaches to identifying and fulfilling your destiny in order to experience God's original intention for the "more than enough" life. The information in this book has power to guarantee true transformation of life and I heartedly recommend it as a potential destiny moulding and life transforming material.

As you read and meditate on this book, I pray it will bring you good success in all your ways. Read it, meditate on it and use the principles.

Dr James Nanjo D.D, DTh
Senior Pastor of Restoration Chapel International

1

Go Now!
Go Get a Dream

I get very excited anytime I have the opportunity to talk about dreams. I don't mean the kind of dream one has when sleeping— seeing cats and dogs or fighting with snakes and lions and so on. No, I mean the dreams that force a man or woman to want to achieve something unique in life. I tell you for a fact, no two dreams are ever the same no matter how hard you force yourself to see the similarity. Another way a dream is looked at is by use of the word *vision*. Whether a person has a dream or a vision, one common factor proves that they mean the same thing: they need to be achieved.

I say "need" here because having a dream is one thing and achieving it is quite another, but whatever the case dreams make any life worth living. It is the dreams that get achieved that become synonymous with visions and purpose. The dreams that do not get achieved will always pretty much remain synonymous with dreams about cats, dogs, snakes, and lions. After all, the latter remains in your head whilst the former is evident for all to see, just as the Bible says in Mathew 5:15 (NKJV):

> *Nor do they light a lamp and put it under a basket, but on a lamp stand and it gives light to all who are in the house."*

Chances are that many of you have already heard about dreams, but let me suggest to you here that a dream is pretty much like a destination. It's been said that "life is a journey." The question we often have not asked ourselves is this - "a journey to where?" Let me add a little more to that and say that a true dream spells out (a) where you want to get to and (b) what you want to achieve or do when you get there. In other words, if you know the destination and what you will be doing at that destination, chances are high that it will be easier for you to figure out the mode of transportation to get there, the type of clothing to wear, and maybe even the kind of food to eat.

See, most people leave it at "where you want to get to," but you must ask yourself – and then what? Let me give you an example: If two brothers A and B were both attending weddings in December, one in Antarctica and the other in a Moroccan desert, this in itself defines their destinations fully. On the one hand, it defines where they want to get to (an extremely cold Antarctica and a very hot Moroccan desert) as well as what they want to do when they get there (attend a wedding). Does it make sense to you when I say that these brothers are likely to have different transportation arrangements? Yes, they may both make use of an airplane at some point, but the final leg of the journeys may see one using a sledge and dogs to travel in ice and snow, whilst the other uses a jeep, camel, or even horse to go through the sandy, windy desert storms.

Consider the way they dress. Chances are that whereas the brother headed for Morocco may prefer a lightweight clothing, brother A heading for Antarctica may need several jumpers or thermal wears to enjoy the wedding comfortably. Did you know that their different destinations will also determine what kind of food they will most likely eat before, during, and after? Think about it. Brother A is likely to need heat-generating food whilst brother B focuses on foods that ensure sufficient levels of fluid are retained in his body. And the fact that they are there to attend a wedding means the chances of seeing them in farm clothes or laboratory robes at the wedding is close to zero right? Surprised? Don't be. The point I am driving home is that your destination and what you will be doing when you get there determine everything else.

Now I feel comfortable to say this: Inherent in every person is a dream. God put it there. If at any point in time you feel restless, unhappy, and unfulfilled in your life's journey, then chances are that you haven't discovered your dream, and as a result you are probably (figuratively speaking) eating the wrong foods, wearing the wrong clothes, and using the wrong transportation modes. If you knew exactly where you were going, chances are even greater that you would stop doing some things you currently find okay doing. You will. It's inherent in us. You don't need someone else to tell you that; just in the same way you don't need someone to tell you that if you wish to be on your knees at 5:30 p.m. today praying for a breakthrough, then you shouldn't be smoking weed and having casual sex at 5:15 p.m.

Here is a deep truth: God, in creating every human being, wired us up specifically according to the dream He placed in us. There is no way a person filled with a dream to be a world-class lawyer will be wired in such a way as to make him a perfect rugby machine. God doesn't make mistakes when it comes to creation. A dream, in effect, is the same as our purpose. It is what determines why you live the way you live. A dream will answer the question of why you are not living the way your next-door neighbour is, because if you decided to live like them, that's your dream's fulfilment going out the window.

The truth however is that some Christians do not live the way "they should," not so much because they don't want to but more often than not because they don't even know why they should. See, God created us in a supernaturally exceptional way – as soon as you identify your dream, your entire being automatically turns on the synchronising software in you so you realise all of a sudden that some things appear right and others wrong— even though you've been doing all of these things prior to you identifying your dream. The things that appear right, appear to be so because when God wired you up with your dreams, He also wired you with the things that need to be done for those dreams to be achieved. The things that start feeling wrong are the things that were not wired into you for the fulfilment of your dreams.

This is effectively what happens following the discovery of your dream: Anytime you carry out or attempt to carry out an action (any action for that matter), for example, getting a tattoo, going to church to pray, or even a thought of cheating somebody, the Spirit of God in you immediately checks your intended action against a list in your dream and vision database called actions that are right to fulfil the dream (just my own term to explain the process), and if your intended action doesn't appear on the list, you'll either feel a very strong conviction of wrong or you will simply know it isn't right – it's the Spirit at work. Listen to Him. On the other hand however, more often than not, if you haven't yet identified your direction, your vision or your dream, pretty much everything seems right to you.

Now that we know the basics, let's get a little deeper. Genesis 1:1-4 (Amp) reads as follows:

> *In the beginning God (prepared, formed, fashioned, and) created the heavens and the earth. The earth was without form and an empty waste and darkness was upon the face of the very great deep. The Spirit of God was*

moving (hovering, brooding) over the face of the waters. And God said, Let there be light; and there was light. And God saw that the light was good (suitable, pleasant) and He approved it; and God separated the light from the darkness.

I want you to follow me to grasp some spiritual insight here. Two points; first, in darkness God created the earth; second point, originally the earth was without form until the Holy Spirit descended and hovered over it, giving it form. Liken this to a mother chicken that broods over her eggs until they are ready to hatch. When the hen lays its eggs, the chicks are in a formless state, or as the Bible passage above states, they are "without form," (just yoke and egg white) but when the hen sits and broods over these eggs, they form into chicks. Is it surprising in contrast, that when broiler hens lay eggs and do not sit and brood over them, the eggs never form into chicks and hence we can have them for breakfast?

But notice an interesting similarity here. The brooding of the Holy Spirit over the earth gave the earth form and shape and life, but it all happened in darkness. All the time the chick is being formed in its shell whilst the mother hen broods over it there is nothing but darkness. Now darkness is the absence of light. So when God said "let there be light" He wasn't producing light for the first time, because we see in verse 2 that He mentions darkness. He wouldn't have mentioned darkness unless He knew about light.

In verse 4 when the Scripture says "and God saw that the light was good," what the writer was truly trying to express from the original interpretation was not that the appearance of the light by itself was good, but rather that after the Spirit had brooded over the earth to give it form (in darkness), when God subsequently called for the light to reveal what He was forming in darkness, He *loved* what He saw. In other words God was excited about what He had been forming in the darkness. Don't worry, the mystery of darkness will come in another book if God wills it. Verse 2 above says darkness was upon the very great deep. When God plants dreams in us at formation, He plants them in our minds and hearts, but Genesis 2:7 tells us that after God created man He breathed the breath of life into his nostrils and man became a living being. This is the early creation of the earth being repeated in man's context – "the very great deep that was formless" referred to in verse 2 of Genesis 1 equates to our mind, where our dreams and purpose in life are deposited. Proverbs 25:3 (RKJ) says this: "*As the heavens for height and the **earth for depth**, so the hearts and **minds** of kings are unsearchable.*"

The plan of God in all of this is as follows: As we nurture the Spirit breathed in us to become stronger, He (the Spirit) broods over the dreams deposited in our minds and hearts (the very great deep) until those formless dreams take on form and then life – all in the darkness of our minds. Yes, just like the Spirit of God brooded over the dark, formless earth and it took form. Is it any surprise now that you may have come across the wise saying "the mind of a man is a very dark place"? I say this in the hope that as you pray to God to identify His perfect dream in your life, you'll understand the need to pray for His Spirit to brood over your mind and heart and bring form, shape, and life to the dream(s) in you so that when it eventually comes out into the light, like God, the world can look and say "it is good and pleasant."

My other reason for sharing all this is to make you understand why in times past when you said to people "I have a dream to do XYZ…" they probably laughed you off. But that is completely understandable. First of all, that dream you were talking to them about resides in your "great deep." It is in the darkest places of your mind and heart. Of course they can't see it. You and God are the only ones who have access to that great deep. No one else can see it. And why is it you alone? Because you are the only one wired to carry it out perfectly. No one else could. Not in a zillion years. That's right; if you have the dream it's because only you can do it.

This latter point is something I want to expand on. And I want to start by asking that for a moment you dwell on the question I am about to ask. We know that God is a very sovereign God; He can use anybody or anything to achieve His sovereign desires as we see in Mathew 3:9 (RKJ):

> *"And do not presume to say to yourselves, We have Abraham for our forefather; for I tell you, God is able to **raise** up descendants for Abraham from these **stones**."*

Here we see Mathew saying to his fellow Jews that if they refuse to accept Christ in order to inherit God's kingdom as true descendants of Abraham, God is able to literally raise descendants for Abraham from stones who will believe on Jesus Christ. Amazing! So the bottom line is God can use anybody and anything. The questions I need you to dwell on now are these: Why did God necessarily have to use Moses to deliver the Israelites? There were many other Israelites at the time, even well-learned rabbis. Why did God use Joshua to take them to the Promised Land? Caleb had the same qualifications. Why were Simon, Andrew, James, and John the fishermen used as great apostles; Jesus could easily have used carpenters, goldsmiths, rabbis, and even shepherds. God indeed is a sovereign God, so why? Are you wondering? The answer is quite simple – only the people He used in all of these examples were perfectly wired for such dreams. God, as we said earlier in this chapter, will only give you a dream He has wired you for. See, God is an omniscient God. In other words He is "all efficient," meaning that by His nature He achieves before He even thinks it. He perfects the product before He even dreams up the need for such a product, which is to say before He put a dream in you, He already wired you to fulfil that dream.

What is the dream in you my fellow heir of Christ? What dream have you been wired for? Think about it, the dream behind the creation of a carpet Hoover is that it would "suck the dirt away," hence it is wired in such a way to perform just that. Another electrical equipment, say the hand dryer, a standing fan, or a convection heater, may be manufactured using the same elements, parts, and materials used for the carpet Hoover, but the only reason why these other equipment cannot do the work of the Hoover is this – they are not wired to be a Hoover. Remember, same elements, same year of manufacture, and maybe even the same manufacturer, yet different dreams for the different equipment.

Most people I talk to concerning dreams have an erroneous opinion that every person should conceive their dreams because this is the only way they can take responsibility for those dreams. Well, I have news for you. Every person's dream is already conceived in him or her when they are created by God, and the beauty of it is that these dreams are not conceived by us, they are conceived by God. It follows reason; it is He who created you the way He did, so it is He who knows perfectly *why* He created you the way He did. Do you know why the nerves in your left arm are shorter or longer than those of the next man or woman sitting next to you in a crowd? Do you know why your ear is shaped the way it is? Do you know why the knuckles on your index finger are the way they are? Do you? Do you think they have anything to do with God wanting you to become an excellent inventor instead of the lawyer *you* want to be? Do you?

I try to explain it like this: Imagine entering an electrical shop (I confess I don't know why I keep using electrical examples) and walking up to a lawnmower on display and the following conversation ensues…

You *(speaking aloud to yourself)*: Hmm, I think I need to buy this lawnmower in order to cut the grass in my back garden.

Lawnmower: Hey! Hold on! Who says I want to cut grass, huh? I have just been manufactured that way, but I'm not really for cutting grass! **You:** What! *(In utter shock and surprise and shaking all over)*

Lawnmower: Listen, stop being so dramatic! Give me a few days, I am trying to conceive my own dream and vision about what I want to achieve in life. Why don't you come back next week Thursday and check if I have decided grass cutting is my life's dream OK? Now off you go."

I bet you would run out of that shop before the conversation even finishes. But the point I am trying to make is this: The manufactured product/the created being does not decide "why" it was created or manufactured; rather it performs to its best what it is created for.

More often than not the reason why we don't like certain products as compared to others is not really because the manufacturers are bad, but because the products for some reason do not perform well the purposes for which they were manufactured. In the same manner when God creates us with a particular dream implanted in us, wires us to perform that and only that dream, and then we go off deciding and working on our own dreams, we are not only faulty products, we are giving God a bad name. I love what Christ Jesus says in John 12:49 (AMP):

> *This is because I have never spoken on my own authority or of my own accord or as self-appointed, but the Father who sent Me* **has Himself given Me orders [concerning] what to say and what to tell.**

Perfect! The truth, my brothers and sisters, is that we all as Christians wish to succeed and possess our gates of elevation and dominion in the world, but we have done so or better still attempted to do so completely ignoring what our God has dreamed us up for. Can't you see that you are giving God a bad name doing the things you are doing, the very things which the Spirit in you keeps saying "this is not you"?

God had a dream when He created you. If it wasn't for that dream, He would not have wired you up the way He did. If you don't know, then let me admonish you; Everything about you right now is in place so you will fulfil the perfect dream God had about you way before His hand touched the clay to form you. Don't you know your fingers, your bone structure, your legs, the way you talk, the way your mind functions, the schools you attended, the education you had or didn't have, the situations you have been through…. Can't you see that everything about you was created and permitted by God to make you the *only* perfect candidate to carry out that dream? Psalm 139:12-17 (AMP) says it so well:

> *Even the darkness hides nothing from You, but the night shines as the day; the darkness and the light are both alike to You. For You did form my inward parts; You did knit me together in my mother's womb. I will confess and praise You for You are fearful and wonderful and for the awful wonder of my birth! Wonderful are Your works, and that my inner self knows right well. My frame was not hidden from You when I was being formed in secret [and] intricately and curiously wrought [as if embroidered with various colours] in the depths of the earth [a region of darkness and mystery]. Your eyes saw my unformed substance, and in Your book all the days [of my life] were written before ever they took shape, when as yet there was none of them. How precious and weighty also are Your thoughts to me, O God! How vast is the sum of them.*

And here is the most amazing truth of all – when God created you and breathed into you, what He breathed in you was every dream in Him concerning you up to the point when He breathed into your nostrils, not only that but everything else that made Him a living God. And that's why in Genesis 2:7 (AMP) the Word says:

> *"Then the Lord God formed man from the dust of the ground and breathed into his nostrils the breath or spirit of life,* **and man became a living being.**"

Have you noticed that man only becomes a living being *after* the breath of the Spirit of Life, the same Spirit that hovered on the face of the deep at the beginning of creation? In fact science has recently proven that the essential chemical elements found in human and animal life are the same as those found in the soil. This scientific fact was not known until recent times. And so just as the earth is known to be able to support all life forms and even make things grow into new life forms, so it is that the dreams God deposited in you should be sustained and made to grow in you.

Everything about you is life-giving, because you carry inside of you the same breath of the Holy Spirit that hovered in the beginning and made the formless earth become a life-sustaining and life giving entity. If you think it was mere coincidence that God waited for the Spirit to hover over the earth before using that same clay (after it had been impregnated with life-sustaining abilities by the Spirit) to form man, then think again. Think deeply again.

He did this so intricately that even your body, on its own knows the dream, your spirit knows the dream, and so does your soul. Deep inside, you know. Believe it or not, you know. You can pretend you don't and you can deliberately ignore it because it is most convenient, but the truth is that you know. Read the Psalm above.

King David came to a point where he could not deny that whatever God's dream was concerning him was already in his total being. In other words, he did not have to look far for it. In Psalm 139:14 quoted above, he specifically says it: *"and my inner self knows very well."* Now let me ask you a question. Have you ever tried your hand at something, say a new job, vocation, hobby, career, habit, or way of reasoning, and realised without anybody telling you that "this is just not me"? Have you? And have you stopped to wonder why? Why is it that other people are so successful at being bankers, accountants, writers, musicians, army generals, and yet you know *within your inner self* that if you tried your hands at any of them, you would not only crash, you would crash miserably? Has it occurred to you that it is because your spirit, your body, and your soul are not wired for any of those dreams?

There is a dream in you, so please go find it.

God's dreams are in you, and I can assure you that it is only in fulfilling these dreams that you can ever begin to live life fully. The first and foremost dream that is a standard dream for every believer is to worship God, just as it is standard for any electrical equipment to have a "switch" even though they have different purposes. Yet they all have switches. The switch is what turns it ON to perform what it was manufactured for.

The reason why a lawnmower was created was so that it can cut the grass for you, but imagine taking the mower to the lawn at the back of your house and, without turning it on, you start pushing it back and forth across the lawn. I can assure you that, until the apocalypse comes, the grass in your lawn will grow and grow and grow. That is what the worship of God is to us as Christians. And I don't mean worshiping God by singing alone; that is just a very small part of it. I mean worshiping Him with our body, soul, and spirit.

If you know or sense you haven't been living in the dream God intended for you, then do what I did first – pray and ask for repentance, because most likely the dream you are living right now is a dream you created for yourself, just like the lawnmower on display in the electrical shop.

Here is a final mystery I want to share with you. You see, God does not change. Hebrews 6:17 (AMP) says:

> *"Accordingly God also, in His desire to show more convincingly and beyond doubt to those who were to inherit the promise the unchangeableness of His purpose and plan, intervened (mediated) with an oath."*

His unchanging nature implies that the dream He had concerning you before He formed you— that which He breathed into you when He formed you and that which He expects you to live now— are all one and the same. Remember the Scripture says in Genesis 2:7 *"and man became a living being."* Well, the dream that God breathed into you was intended from the beginning by God to become and continue to be living. Your identification and fulfilment of (or walking in) God's divine dream for your life becomes a testimony in itself that "God is a living God." In order words, if God is truly a living God and everything He does is for ever, then it makes sense that His dream deposited in you should forever live, by being fulfilled in you. If on the other hand, His dream in you is not being fulfilled, or brought to life in you or to put it bluntly, is dead, then effectively, you are bearing witness to the fact that "God is a dead God".

The truth is, if we as Christians are walking in purposes other than what God has wired us for, then effectively what we are telling the world is "I think my God had it all mixed up by wiring me in a way that is not fit for MY dream." Or better still, our inability to walk in God's purposed dream for us, which is in us, is another way of us thumping our chest and saying to the world, "You know what, I think God was daydreaming when He had all those dreams about me at creation. I can't believe He would even think of me being what He dreamt me to be! Gosh, He got it all messed up! Unbelievable, this God of ours…ha ha ha."

The questions, my friends, are these: They are ones that everyone must answer truthfully for themselves. I ask of my God, the true and only God, Creator, and possessor of heaven and earth, that His Spirit will lead you into all truth as you answer these questions, for out of the truth of those answers your own personal revelation about God's purposed dream for your life will come forth:

1. What are you doing now or thinking about doing? What dreams are you living?

2. Did you ever talk to God about the dream you are living now? (Proverbs 3:6)

3. Really? What did He say then? (Deuteronomy 5:24)

4. Is your spirit, body, and soul excited about and in tune with living your current dream? Do you feel in your innermost self and not just in your mind that this is right? (Psalm 139:14)

5. If not, what would your innermost self be excited about?

6. Do you have to struggle to do or live your current dream? What then is it that you don't struggle to do or live? What comes to you naturally? What does your heart, spirit, and soul, feel happy doing?

7. What is it that when you start doing, thinking about, or living, your spirit and soul really feel a free flow? What is it that you can do, think about, or live your entire life doing over and over again and still want to do more?

8. Have you inquired of God? What has He repeatedly said to you in dreams, visions, prophecies, wisdom, and the whisperings of His Spirit? What have you heard over and over again and ignored? As you read through the pages of this chapter, what kept coming to you? Why do you think He created you the way He did? Take every single part of your entire being one by one and ask yourself the same question for each of them.

9. If you are not successful in achieving your dream and making an impact, then what is your proof to the unbeliever that God has made a difference in your life?

10. Finally: What is your God-given dream? (Don't worry if you haven't found it yet. You will, by the time you are done reading this book. By the Spirit of God.)

PRAYER POINTS:

1. Pray to God through Jesus Christ asking for forgiveness for having followed your self-ordained dreams and purposes and, by so doing, giving God a bad reputation.

2. Pray to the Lord Jesus that as you go through this searching journey your reasoning mind will be put to rest and the mind of your spirit will be awakened.

3. Pray for the Holy Spirit to lead you into all truth concerning the dream and purpose God created you for.

4. Pray and ask the Holy Spirit to hover over your mind and stir up life in the dream and purpose God deposited in you at creation and give it "form."

5. Pray and ask God for a quickened discernment and a quickened ear to hear the Holy Spirit when He speaks to you concerning your God-given dream(s).

6. Pray to Jesus for the spirit of humility to follow the leading of His Spirit and not to be headstrong. Remember, what God has ordained, He will provide for. You may be doing so well in "your own" dream right now that you'll think it is really the dream God purposed for you. Is it really?

7. Thank God for His grace and mercy, that even as you have called Him by His name and humbled yourself and made a U-turn, He is kind enough to set you up anew and afresh. Also thank Him for His kindness to help you recover all the lost years.

2

Look in Your Hand
—That's All You Need

Each of us at some point in our lives has desired to move a step further from where we are. Whether in a professional, private business, or personal capacity, there is likely to have come a point when you felt "flat" or "stale" or "unfulfilled" in your current state and with a corresponding desire to move a step forward. This corresponding desire is a very natural essence of our godly nature.

When God created man, He embedded in him the supernatural ability to function both in the earth realm and in the heaven realm. He was naturally able to flow between natural and supernatural. Unlike modern-day man-after-the-fall, he didn't have to make any effort to switch intermittently between spirit and flesh. It was almost the same to be in the flesh (by which he had a connection with the earth) and to be in the spirit (by which he had a connection with heaven). This ability to live in both realms as though it were one brought man to a state of supernatural evolution where the way he felt on earth was as intricately *normal* as the way he felt when communing with God in the heavenly realm.

After the fall, however, there was pretty much a "break in transmission" of that equilibrium, and man was for a time restricted to the earthly realm. Yet this restriction did not take away man's desire to connect to the higher realm. Note that this desire was not one that man developed over time—no, that would be a habit and in some cases an addiction, not a desire per se. Rather, it was an innate desire that formed part of his DNA, just like the natural desire to thirst after water or hunger after food.

Now ask yourself, how possible would it be for anyone to deny you of the desire to thirst after water or hunger after food? Close to impossible right? Well, that's exactly why man can never stop desiring to aspire to greater heights and to perfection. It is the same state of greatness and perfection that formed a natural part of his DNA from the time man was created, so if it is hard enough to stop desiring water or food, you can bet your last dime it is more than just hard to stop desiring to rise to greater heights – the heavenly height of perfection. It is simply man's desire to be restored back to the state he was originally created to exist in and to the state he was used to existing in before the great Adamic fall.

Some sceptical Christians may argue "Oh yeah? Well, that desire to reach higher heights was a natural thing for Adam, but not us." Here is a truth you may want to consider, a truth that runs throughout the Bible and even more practically in ordinary life. When the first man Adam was created, we were all in him. God did not create Adam and then everybody else with him. The original intent as I gather by revelation is that as Adam evolved supernaturally, every seed that came out of him would bear the same properties and characteristics of Adam up to the point of his evolvement. Thus up to the point when Adam left the garden and started to procreate, he had evolved to the point of 1) having been naturally accustomed to operating in both earthly and heavenly realms and 2) having lost this ability to operate in the two realms. This loss meant he had unsatisfied desires to be restored back to the higher heavenly realm.

Why this desire? Well, when food is available, you don't always hunger for it as much as when it's taken from you, right? It's the same thing. When the ability to function simultaneously in both realms was taken from Adam, his desire for higher and more perfected things increased. It therefore is no surprise, judging from the level Adam evolved to before he started procreating, that we also, without prompting have a natural urge in us to strive toward perfection.

Take Abraham for an example. Ishmael and Isaac were both seeds already in his loins when he received the promise of God in Genesis 12.1-3 (AMP).

> *NOW [in Haran] the Lord said to Abram, Go for yourself [for your own advantage] away from your country, from your relatives and your father's house, to the land that I will show you.* ***And I will make of you a great nation, and I will bless you [with abundant increase of favours] and make your name famous and distinguished, and you will be a blessing [dispensing good to others].*** *And I will bless those who bless you [who confer prosperity or happiness upon you] and curse him who curses or uses insolent language toward you; in you will all the families and kindred of the earth be blessed [and by you they will bless themselves].*

Realistically speaking, at the point when Ishmael was born, he had access to this promise given to Abram by God because he was ***inside and a part of*** Abram when it was given. If you doubt this, reread verse 2 of the chapter just quoted above (Genesis 12:2) and now move fast forward and read the blessing that God Himself uttered concerning Ishmael in Genesis 17:20 (AMP), which reads:

> "And as for Ishmael, I have heard and heeded you: behold, **I will bless him and will make him fruitful and will multiply him exceedingly**; He will be the father of twelve princes, **and I will make him a great nation.**"

Can you identify the exact same blessing that was promised to Abram being delivered to Ishmael also? "To bless him and make him a great nation." The exact same promise was fulfilled in Ishmael's destiny as it was in [Abram's] Abraham's. Why? Because Ishmael was in Abram when that promise was received.

Now that we understand why we aspire to greater and more perfect things, let us proceed further and deal with the main reason for this chapter. I do not believe there has ever been a problem with us as children of God desiring great things. As we've seen, we were used to it at a point and it has been imbedded in our DNA. The problem for us modern-day Christians is the route we have taken to satisfy our inner desire to achieve higher.

Over and over again we have wrongly believed that in order to achieve higher goals and desires in our lives, we *need* to add something more to us. So it is no surprise that with this false belief Christian women, for example, see nothing wrong with distorting their God-given beauty by adding something extra through surgery; men and women in professions believe they need to take more degrees, more courses, embark on more training programs before they can achieve the heights they want to reach. I am not saying it is wrong to gain more education and knowledge.

I used to think the same way too. I was a professional accountant, and at the age of thirty-three I decided my life was getting stale and that I wasn't getting as much of a kick from figures, numbers, and balance sheets as I did when I started off.

Guess what my first move was? I registered for another professional course. Yeah, great! I am not by any means saying that one does not need to develop themselves if that is indeed the right path to ply. I'll be the first to say that when you identify your talent in a niche area, you need to develop that talent and keep it on the cutting edge at all times. What I am saying is that in more than eighty per cent of the cases where we earnestly want to move higher in life, the first thing we should do is not add something to ourselves, but rather ask ourselves "What do you have in your hand?"

In other words, when you get to the point where you genuinely desire to see your life rise to a higher pedestal, what you need in order to get to that new and higher level is already in your hand.

At the point when I decided accounting was not cutting it for me anymore, like I said, my first logical action was to register for a variant professional course. It was still something to do with accounting (can you believe that?) though a little different, but God had His own plans for me. And by the divine mercy of God, He led me into some very, very deep truths. I had come back from work one of those many boring days, didn't feel like eating, watching TV, or doing anything, but thank God for the Holy Spirit. He led me to the book of Exodus and the commissioning of Moses for the redemption of the children of Israel.

Here is a great truth I wish to share with you. Moses had worked for Jethro, his father-in-law, for forty years as a shepherd.

Now as a shepherd, your most important tool is your staff, or as Moses referred to it, your rod. A shepherd's staff or rod in those days was pretty much an all-purpose tool. He used it to guide his flock, to pull them out of ditches, to hit or correct the "sheep behaving badly." But that was not all. A shepherd's rod was also used to fight—both to defend the shepherd's own life and the life of his flock—and as a symbol of identity to differentiate say a shepherd from a carpenter.

Now here is one of the exciting aspects to it all: If Moses had served as a shepherd for forty years, he was more than familiar with his rod. His hands were used to holding it. At the time when he encountered the burning bush in Exodus 3, he was very used to having his rod with him and, I dare say, excellent at using it for every intended purpose. Take a look at Exodus 4:1-5 (AMP) with me:

> *AND MOSES answered, But behold, they will not believe me or listen to and obey my voice; for they will say, The Lord has not appeared to you. And the Lord said to him,* ***what is that in your hand? And he said a rod****. And He said, Cast it on the ground. And he did so and it became a serpent [the symbol of royal and divine power worn on the crown of the Pharaohs]; and Moses fled from before it. And the Lord said to Moses Put forth your hand and take it by the tail. And he stretched out his hand and caught it, and it became a rod in his hand, [This you*

shall do, said the Lord] that the elders may believe that the Lord, the God of their fathers, of Abraham, of Isaac, and of Jacob, has indeed appeared to you.

Check this out: When God asked Moses "what is that in your hand?" notice what Moses' response was—"a rod." English language teaches us that there is a difference between saying "an elephant" and "the elephant." The former denotes some degree of non-identity; in other words, it is just an ordinary elephant and it could also be anybody's elephant whereas the latter gives it some specific identity, an identity known to persons other than the person speaking. Saying "the elephant" indicates that this particular elephant is known. It is not just out there but rather it can be pinpointed as having a particular characteristic, it is one that everybody else can relate to. It wasn't that God did not know what was already in Moses' hand. No, He wanted to see if Moses knew the value of the one thing he had used every day since he started shepherding forty years earlier. He said **"a rod."** He did not say "the rod" or better still "my rod"; instead he said **"a rod."**

This unfortunately is the case with most of us who genuinely desire to rise higher above our current circumstances and find fulfilment in our life's purposes. The first thing we do consciously and unconsciously on our journeys to change our lives is ignore the very things we have in our hands. We get so familiar with them that we cannot fathom why or even how those same parts of us can be used to bring us fulfilment and a turnaround in our circumstances.

Let me take you even deeper. Moses was a shepherd before his calling, and there were many other tools he would have used in his job. He very likely would have used knives to slaughter sheep, a horn to call them to gather, and a whole lot of other things, but the truth is that he used the rod a lot more times and in a lot of different ways. God did not just decide that very moment that He was going to use Moses' rod as His authority upon Moses. God knew He was going to use something that Moses was excellent at handling. God placed His authority on Moses' rod not because it was the only thing he had, but because Moses was so excellent at using that rod to correct, to guide, to lead, to defend, and to identify with his sheep. Exactly the same job description Moses was given concerning bringing the children of Israel out of Egypt.

There are areas of our lives that we have exercised and developed so much that if we were to use those areas of our lives the way Moses later used the rod, we very likely would have done better than Moses. I remember a little boy who from the age of four used to run around the family compound all the time. All through his growth his legs were always moving. He was always walking and running. There was just something about using his legs that made him comfortable and excited. Would you be surprised to find that after this young man eventually took on the sport of soccer, he became one of the most respected, swiftest and most agile wingers I have ever seen? His legs were his rod. What is your rod?

The passage quoted above also reflects how when God heard the answer that Moses gave Him, He further instructed Moses to throw the rod on the ground. The Scripture says the rod turned into a snake; God asked Moses to pick it up by the tail and it turned back into a rod. I submit to you by revelation that if Moses had already figured out the value of the rod in his hand, God would not have gone through this extra process. God had to force Moses to see the rod differently. He had to force Moses to see that it really was not just a rod in his hand, but rather a part of God that nobody else of the multitude of Israel had. Moses indeed had to throw the rod on the ground. He had to let it leave his hand and then stand back so he could see what he had really been holding all this while.

The rod turning into a snake was God communicating to Moses in a language he would better understand. Why? Moses knew he was being sent back to Pharaoh, and in fact he himself used to be in the palace of Pharaoh, educated and schooled in the highest mystical schools of the civilisation at the time. Moses knew that in the palace of Pharaoh the symbol of authority and power was the snake. God turned the rod into a snake so that Moses could identify that what he thought was ordinary, what he thought he was used to and did not carry any essence, what he thought was just "a rod" was in fact of greater essence than he imagined.

Look in Your Hand—That's All You Need

Note three major things that happened here. Moses threw the rod in front of him, indicating that he stepped back to take a second look at what he used to think was a normal stick in his hand. It was an opportunity God gave Moses to see the rod the way He (God) saw it. Sometimes that is exactly what we all need to do—take a step back and reconsider the things we have, the things we use and do every day and which we have become so excellent at using and doing *but* which unfortunately we ignore or brush aside and do not consider as our prized rods of greatness. How do you see the rod in your hand? Do you see it the same way God does, or do you still see it as just "a rod"? You still think it's an ordinary rod?

A second thing happened: When Moses threw the rod on the ground God's power came on it, indicating how God's blessing comes upon the rod we identify in our hands once we lay it before Him. But the critical thing is that we have to willingly do as He orders us and lay it before Him. Moses would never have seen the power in the rod if he hadn't first laid it before God. Proverbs 3:6 (AMP) says,

> *"In all your ways know, recognize, and acknowledge Him, and He will direct and make straight and plain your paths."*

By this act, Moses was recognizing and acknowledging God's direction in his new understanding of what other powers were in the rod, and furthermore how to even hold it – mind you God asked him to grab it "by the tail."

The third and final occurrence in the unfolded event was that Moses took back the rod into his hand. It was still his rod, but he had just been educated in the true nature and power of this rod. Besides all that, he remained the one person who had optimal ability in the use of that rod; after all, it was his rod.

Just to side track a little, did you notice that the tail of the snake Moses held when he was picking it up became the head of the rod in his hand? Start thinking now. If you are not thinking, then please read it again. To reiterate, did you notice that the tail of the snake Moses picked up from the ground became the head of the rod in his hand? Think about this for a minute: Snakes are usually held by the head so that they don't turn around and bite you, so to start with, it was a very dangerous thing for Moses to be holding the snake by the tail. This is common knowledge right? Good.

The other generally accepted truth (or should I say, lie) in the earth is that the head is better or mightier than the tail. In other words, between the two, the tail was the weakest. But notice that it was this same tail that became the head of a stiff rod in Moses' hand. And the message? There are things that are a part of us (just like the rod was a daily part of Moses) which are strong in our hands (just like the rod was used by Moses in everything) but which if we allow people to define it (just like the rod of Moses was laid horizontal on the earth), they will not only make it look deadly, unprofitable, poisonous, untamed, and disgusting (just like the rod he knew for most of his life becoming a deadly thing to run away from), but they (the people of the earth) would also erroneously have us believe that what we know to be the head is really the tail and what we know to be the tail is really the head (just like what appeared to be tail of the snake was actually the head of Moses' rod).

If Moses had followed the lies of the earth and picked up the snake by the head (after all the head is considered the safest and strongest part) he would have ended up holding his "own" rod by the tail (upside down and thereby circumventing his own power) – even though it was his own rod. And if you don't remember anything, remember this: The only cardinal point at which the rod becomes a snake, the snake becomes a rod, the tail becomes the head, and the head becomes the tail is the earth. It all happens when it touches the earth or is taken from the earth. The rod will always be "your rod" when it is in "your hands." I repeat, when it is in "your hands," when you "cast it" or "throw it down" to the earth (before people), it will become something even you will run away from. And so is the talent in you, God's diamond on earth. Yeah! I know you smiled at that one.

After all of this happening, notice what profundity the Bible attributes to the same rod that Moses originally referred to as "a rod" in Exodus 4:20 (AMP):

> *"And Moses took his wife and his sons and set them on donkeys, and he returned to the land of Egypt; and Moses took **the rod of God** in his hand."*

After God touched the rod, after Moses saw the rod in the same way God saw it, the Bible now refers to the same rod as "the rod of God in his hand."

I ask of God that by the time you finish reading this book you will not only identify "the rod of God" in your hand but also see the essential need of laying it before Him and allowing His Holy Spirit to open the eyes of your understanding, that you should see the rod in your hand the way He sees it. And I assure you that when this happens, your journey to move from your current unhappy life to a pleasant more perfected one—from the wilderness to the palace; from Egypt to your promised destiny—will be filled with great and mighty works.

If your rod cannot be called the rod of God, then my advice to you is do not yet even start the journey. The rod that you have laid before God; the rod that you allow God to strengthen and empower; the rod whose abilities you understand through the eyes of God—this will be the rod that swallows the rods of your Pharaoh, opens your Red Seas when your enemies come after you, and provides you with water in the wilderness when you thirst and healing when you are broken.

In order to end this chapter well, I'd like to ensure your understanding of why you need to identify the abilities inherent in you that can give you victory and success in life. I wish to finally lure you to the remarkable story of David as a youth and his defeat of Goliath. A few things happened that bear semblance to the treatise above on Moses' encounter with God and how "a rod" became "the rod of God." In the run-up to the Goliath encounter, we see David in the army camp of Israel demanding to know what the prize is for the man who kills Goliath (1 Samuel 17:25) and how he was told of great riches, the king's daughter in marriage, and eternal exemption from taxes.

Now, these were desires of perfection that David aspired to. Remember that even though he had been anointed at this stage, he was still shepherding his father's flock. This desire to rise above our current circumstances to a more perfect life is inherent in all of us humans, including Christians. Ever wonder why no one has to be schooled in order to know what they aspire to? It's already in our DNA. First Samuel 17:34-37 (AMP) paints a picture that shares some thoughts on David as follows:

> *"And David said to Saul, Your servant kept his father's sheep. And when there came a lion or again a bear and took a lamb out of the flock, I went out after it and **smote** it and delivered the lamb out of its mouth; and when it arose against me, I caught it by its beard and **smote** it and killed it. Your servant killed both the lion and the bear; and this uncircumcised Philistine shall be like one of them, for he has defied the armies of the living God!*

> *David said, The Lord Who delivered me out of the paw of the lion and out of the paw of the bear, He will deliver me out of the hand of this Philistine. And Saul said to David, Go, and the Lord be with you!"*

In the shepherding life of David, there was one item that formed an everyday part of him— his sling. In other words, that was his rod. His sling was what he was so used to, so excellent at using. It was the one thing whose use was second nature to him. We know that slings can be best used when the target is a distance away. But David had mastered the use of his sling so intimately that he could even use it on a target at a hair's distance away. So in verse 35 he says he could actually hold a lion by the beard (he surely must be pretty close to do that) and still strike it with the sling. When the text says he "smote it," it implies the use of a hard object, or in this case a stone in the sling. The word "smote" used in this context comes from the Hebrew word *machat* which translates as "shatter through" indicating that anytime he used the sling against wild animals, the stone in the sling shattered through the animals' skulls.

From the way David talks about his smiting ability, it is obvious that he was very skilful with the sling. By this time he would have become so natural in its use that he felt sure about its effect and its results. This is one of the differences between Moses and David. In the case of David, he knew his rod (sling) very well, even to the extent that he knew its "shatter through" capabilities. I perceive that if God had asked David "what is that in your hand?" a likely answer would have been *"this is **my sling** with which I smote lions and bears and many terrible beasts that tried to eat my father's sheep."*

In verse 37 David stresses, without mincing words, that the Lord is with him (and for that matter with his sling also), hence the reason for his past and future conquests with his sling. Here lies another fundamental difference between how David saw his sling and Moses his rod. To David it was not an ordinary sling; he saw it through the eyes of the Lord. His understanding was that if it wasn't for the Lord, the sling would not be useful. Moses on the other hand had to throw his rod down for God to touch it and turn it into a serpent before he was able to see what his rod could become once it was in his hand and under the power of the Lord.

So there it is; in the case of both men, God used the one thing in their hands that they were so used to handling, excellent at applying, and perfect at identifying with. God, in turning your life upward to a greater perfection, would more than likely use something you already have in your hand. Something you have used for so long. Something you are so used to, something you have naturally mastered, yet something you have all this while considered trivial. Today I ask you this question:

"What is that in your hand?"

Let me end on a least expected revelation. One of the definitions of the word *dominion* is "a supposed higher order of angels." That's what the academics say, but the truth is that we, who are created in the likeness and possessing the Spirit of God, are the "supposed higher order of angels." So by definition, as a child of God and a believer, you should automatically bear the name "dominion." Now let me deal with that little doubt hanging in your head as to whether you are a higher-order angel (above ordinary angels) or not. Please answer these questions truthfully, even with the minimal amount of reasoning:

1. The Bible says in Mathew 7:10 that even amongst us humans, if a child asks his father for fish, he won't be given a snake. How much more if we as believers ask from God? My question is this: Do you believe that God will feed human beings with food that should be eaten by termites? In other words, do you believe God will make the "mistake" of feeding you with wood instead of bread?

2. Do you believe that Jesus, in order to communicate with us from heaven, sent us the Holy Spirit (John 16:13)? Now if you believe that, do you also believe that with Jesus seated in heaven at the right hand of God, He is

communicating (the Hebrew uses the word *confessing*) with God and angels concerning us? The Bible talks about deep calling unto deep, and I believe in that respect that Christ in heaven is only communicating (or confessing) to God and angels on matters that are on the same higher level as God and His angels. Do you agree to this?

3. Finally, do you believe that you can only talk to men in the language of men? Do you believe it is close to impossible to talk to a human being in the language of an insect? Note that even though human beings and insects are classified as part of the animal kingdom, their different levels in that kingdom make it impossible for either of them to speak or understand each other's communication. True or False?

Is there meaning to all these analogies? Yes, one! Only things created on the same plane can understand each other's language. Now in the same order, consider these:

1. Psalm 78:25 says God fed men with the food of angels. You don't genuinely think God was making a mistake do you? Moses ate manna in the wilderness, the food of angels, but the apostles ate something not even angels have eaten before: They ate the body of Christ and drank

of His blood, but they ate of Him and drank of Him whilst He was here on earth. We today, as advanced believers, have eaten more than angels and the apostles; we eat the communion, the holy body and blood of Christ, whilst He is being represented on the right hand of God. In effect, we are eating of divinity. (Do you have any idea what the communion holds? When Christ said "do this in remembrance of Me," the idea was that anytime we partake of this holy act, we are digesting divinity into our beings—everything His body and blood was capable of)

2. Luke 12:8 talks about Christ "confessing" us to the angels of God. Now surely you and I must be highly esteemed creations for Christ in heaven to have a conversation about us with angels. Think about it, when the president of the United States of America meets the prime minister of Great Britain, they are most likely not going to be talking about a farm boy who was standing on the street when the president's convoy was passing through a street somewhere in Africa on his last visit; they are most likely (if they should ever have a conversation about a person), talk about another president or prime minister or someone of similar importance. So think about it. If Christ will be confessing you to angels in heaven, He surely must consider you on the same plane as Himself and the angels. Are you thinking?

3. In 1 Corinthians 13:1, Paul talks about speaking "in tongues" as the language of angels. Now you tell me from point 3 above (in the earlier list) how we can speak a language of angels unless we are on the same plane of operation as angels or higher (in this case)? You tell me.

I have said all the above to lead you into an even deeper understanding of revelation. The Bible says in Colossians 1:16 (AMP):

"For it was in Him that all things were created, in heaven and on earth, things seen and things unseen, whether thrones, dominions, rulers, or authorities; all things were created and exist through Him [by His service, intervention] and in and for Him."

Most often when Christians read the words "thrones, dominions or principalities, rulers, authorities" we immediately associate these with the several levels of demonic and satanic operations. Yes that's true. But the even greater truth is that these are also levels of supernatural positions for the people of God. In fact, nothing the devil does is original. Everything he does is an evil duplication of what already exists in God's kingdom (remember satan is a disgruntled and dismissed employee who is only using what he learnt whilst he served in God's employment). In other words, we as children of God, filled with the Holy Spirit, should actually also be referred to as **thrones** (because in Revelation 3:21 and Luke 22:30 we are seated with Christ in His Kingdom representing thrones); as **dominions** (because in Genesis 1:26, God formed us in His image and gave us dominion over the air and over all the earth and every creeping thing in it – remember satan was accursed into a creeping serpent. In Psalm 8:5-7 also, God gave us dominion and subjected everything under our feet); as **powers** (because in 2 Timothy 1:7 and Luke 9 God gave us the Spirit of Power); and finally, as **authorities** (because in Luke 10:19 Christ gave us authority to trample on serpents and scorpions, and over all the power of the enemy).

Now, here is the revelation – we can only walk in these various levels and dimensions of power if we allow God to breathe upon everything that is in us and in our hands. Let me break it down for you.

Moses, before he was exiled, attended the best schools of the pharaohs of Egypt. He understood magic, the powers of the sun, the powers of the moon, and all the other powers that worked in the earth. He knew the magicians in the palace had rods like his (before the encounter with God), and I am certain he knew the powerful magical powers that the magicians' rods possess when he was in Egypt. That is why when God asked him "what is that in your hand" he was quick to say "a rod." I believe Moses made a quick comparison between his rod at the time and the power he knew the magicians of Egypt had in their rods, and hence his conclusion: "a rod." But when he laid the rod on the ground and

God breathed upon that rod, it became as the Bible later refers to it, "the rod of God."

Pharaoh was both a "ruler" and a "principality" – on the dark side of things. But after Moses encountered God, everything he said stood as a law. In other words, everything he said happened whether Pharaoh agreed to it or not. Moses also became a ruler, a principality, and a power on the God side of things. The moment he picked up that rod which God had breathed upon, he picked up the authority to act as God and therefore became a "principality." The dictionary defines principality as "the ruling authority of a prince." Here is what Exodus 7:1 (AMP) has to say:

> *"THE LORD said to Moses, Behold, I make you as God to Pharaoh [to declare My will and purpose to him]; and Aaron your brother shall be your prophet."*

All it took Moses to gain the authority to rule over Pharaoh and Egypt was to have access to the presence of God in order to lay down his rod for God to breathe upon. Are you a believing Christian? Then I can assure you, you already have access to the throne of the most High God. Now lay down your rod, let God breathe over it, and then go forth and take authority and become a God to your pharaohs. But first you must lay down your rod before God

Finally, I ask you again – what is that in your hand?

1. What do you have: "a rod," "the rod," or "my rod"?
2. Do you see the power in your rod the way God sees it?
3. If not, are you willing to lay it down before God that He might show you what power it holds, how to use it, and still make it a part of you?
4. Break away from familiarity. You have always had your rod, so what?
5. Submit your rod to God and let His blessings come upon it.
6. Remember, now it is "the rod of God." It is no more "a rod."
7. Go out and use your rod; it is the power of God in your hands.
8. This is true dominion.
9. This is true authority

Practically speaking, what do you have in your hands – is it your ability to teach or speak, is it your arguing skills, is it your ability to analyse? Are you mechanically inclined, or do you always bubble with new ideas? Are you very convincing no matter the subject matter, do you have a depth of knowledge of the Word of God, are you gifted to raise deep soul-stirring praise and worship? Do you have the ability to be domestic or to serve? Do you manage other people well? Are you a fighter, or maybe inspiring people comes naturally to you, or encouraging, caring for the sick, or defending the weak and unfortunate? Or maybe you are just good at making money and multiplying it. I could go on and on and on, but really…what exactly is the rod in your hand?

PRAYER POINTS:

1. Pray asking God's forgiveness for having perceived His rod in your hand as merely "a rod."

2. Pray that the stronghold of familiarity be broken over you so that you can begin to look into your life with God's possibilities.

3. Pray to God thanking Him for opening your understanding about what you have in your hand.

4. Pray asking the Lord to give you the spirit of obedience to be able to lay your rod before Him so that He might empower it and cause His authority to come upon it.

5. Pray asking God to give you discernment about people who may attempt to mislead you with respect to the strengths of your rod.

6. Ask the Lord that the same blessings He poured out on your dream(s) will be poured out on your rod also so that the dream for which He created you will be fulfilled for His glory.

7. Finally ask God to fill you with the awareness that the rod of God in your hands has given you the authority to become a power and a ruler.

3

God Was Ready for You a Long Time Ago

So you have a dream, which from a corporate perspective is called a vision – this is what you want the company to achieve. It is that mental picture of where in the future the company will be, will be doing, will be known for, etc. And then next you identify your rod, your niche expertise or product. This is what you or the company have to offer. It is the one thing the rest of the country or world wants because you or the company is the only one who does this product or provides this service the best way. Of course they are all willing to buy it from you because you are the only one who does it best.

Everyone you ever meet who is willing to part with their one dollar or one pound or one unit of any currency will do so to get the best value for their money. Why do you think a man with one dollar and faced with a choice of two similar mobile phones will prefer to buy model A over B? Because apart from the fact that both phones can make it possible for him to send and receive calls, mobile phone A will allow him to listen to the radio also. Yes, same products, same costs, but one gives him more for his dollar than the other. That's why he would buy A and not B.

Back to the analogy I was developing. You have a vision (your God-given dream) and your product or service you wish to use to attain that vision (your God-given rod). You need resources right? You need resources to help you get your product to the many people who need it, to promote it, and to develop it further so that it becomes more valuable beyond just ordinary. I could go on and on, but the bottom line is that you need resources.

It's fascinating how whenever I talk about resources, the first thing that comes to people's mind is "money" and physical money for that matter. It's OK, we are in a materialistic world and money does answer to many things. But I wish to bring your attention to a truly divine understanding that once grasped will revolutionize your thinking. God from the beginning never created money, He created man. Here is a revelation I want you to catch, so please follow me closely. God created men, men created money. Money is man's expression of worth and wealth; man is God's expression of worth and wealth. God owns man, man owns money. Mathew 21:22 (AMP) says:

> "They said, Caesar's. Then He said to them, Pay therefore to Caesar the things that are due to Caesar, and pay to God the things that are due to God."

Jesus was teaching His disciples that money is for men and that they ought to be above money. In other words, give back to Caesar in the form of taxes the money he created and which he considers as wealth, and give back to God the souls of men through their salvation, which God considers as great wealth. Someone will be quick to say, "But the word *men* was not mentioned in the text above." True, but the pretext (and I think you should read this for yourself) teaches that Jesus asked a question first, and the question in its original translation reads "in whose image was the coin made?" and they said Caesar's. It therefore follows that if Jesus had asked the same question about man—"*in whose image was man made?*"—the answer would have been…God! It wouldn't have been hard then to understand why He would have said to His disciples *"give back the souls of men to God because they belong to God."* I tell you no lie, this is the very reason He told them from the beginning "*I will make you fishers of men.*"

In fact all along He was trying to teach them that God in His wisdom in the beginning gave dominion to man over all the earth and the living creatures of the earth. And the essence of that dominion was that man would in turn have dominion over everything that ever came out from the earth. Now tell me, if you owned a piece of land with the rights and documentation to it, don't you think you would also claim any diamonds or gold that was discovered in that parcel of land? I read about an old farmer in the United Kingdom who inherited a farm handed down to him by his father and, before that, his father's father. It so happened that a medieval artefact hunter with a metal detector once passing through his farm discovered a huge treasure of Roman artefacts worth millions. The farmer didn't have to struggle to share in that finding. His ownership of the land automatically entitled him to a greater chunk of the millions valued on the find.

As I said earlier, and on a more profound note, Jesus was really teaching His disciples that they were above money. See, money, in whatever form, shape, colour, or constitution, came from the earth. If it is gold, it came from the earth; if it is paper money, it came from trees in the earth. Think about it, every form of money imaginable comes from the earth. So now can you understand why God was emphasising dominion over the earth rather than the things that came from the earth? Galatians 5:16 (AMP) states:

> *"But I say walk and live [habitually] in the [Holy] Spirit; then you will certainly not gratify the cravings and **desires** of the **flesh** (of human nature without God)."*

Simply put, it means if you have dominion over your flesh, you will be living more in the Spirit. This is no different from all I have been saying above. Why? Because the flesh is made from dust, which is the earth. So when God in the beginning said have dominion over the earth, He also meant dominion over the flesh which was created out of the earth. Let me ask you a question – can you figure out by now why God wants us to live more in the Spirit than in the flesh? Don't worry, I have all day; I am listening.

Quite simply, the Spirit can lead us to all things as in John 14:26. The Holy Spirit can lead us to the things we will ever need. The Holy Spirit led Jesus Christ to find money in the belly of a fish. If you are obedient to the same Holy Spirit that led Christ to do this overcoming act, there is no way He will not lead you to your wealth, your resources, and your riches. Truth is, the Holy Spirit does not have the same limitations as the human brain. That's why if you amplify Him over the fleshly brain, you won't have to think hard about where to find or access resources; He will lead you to it.

Wait! Let me light up your mind just a little here. We have agreed that everything used as money or valued in this world as wealth comes from the earth right? Good! We have also established that the Holy Spirit hovered (brooded) over the face of the entire earth at the beginning of creation right? Good! Before the Holy Spirit's brooding process the whole earth was without form and in chaos. By the time He finished brooding, He had put everything in the earth in its perfect place. That's why He knows where everything is. He arranged the whole earth into "order" so He knows exactly where he put everything. He literally has an inventory list of everything in the earth.

In Mathew 17:24-27 (AMP) a remarkable story unfolds:

> *When they arrived in Capernaum, the collectors of the half shekel [the temple tax] went up to Peter and said, Does not your Teacher pay the half shekel? He answered, Yes. And when he came home, Jesus spoke to him [about it] first, saying, What do you think, Simon? From whom do earthly rulers collect duties or tribute—from their own sons or from others not of their own family? And when Peter said, from other people not of their own family, Jesus said to him, Then the sons are exempt. However, in order not to give offense and cause them to stumble [that is, to cause them to judge unfavourably and unjustly] go down to the sea and throw in a hook. Take the first fish that comes up, and when you open its mouth you will find there a shekel. Take it and give it to them to pay the temple tax for Me and for yourself.*

How on earth would Jesus have known that at that very moment, in the sea, a hook thrown would catch one fish out of the billions swimming in it and that there would be money in the belly of that very first fish? How? Tell me how else if it was not the Holy Spirit. And the fascinating thing is this: It was exactly the amount needed to pay for both His and Peter's taxes. Stop looking at the ceiling or the sky – the answer isn't there!

We started off by saying that money was created by man and man was created by God. **Money in itself is NOT the greatest resource; People are.** The problem we encounter is that in looking for resources, we always end up looking for money rather than people. And ladies, please don't be offended. I am using "man" here as generically referring to both men and women. A simple analogy would have sufficed – if men create money, then if you found men, wouldn't you have found money?

In this world and for the rest of eternity there are going to be two ways of doing things: the system of the world and the system of God. In the God system, people are the resources you need. In the world system, money is the resource you need. But check this out. All the money ever made, all the money being made, and all the money that will ever be made has always and will always be done through man. It's always through people. Money cannot make itself and money doesn't exist on its own. It is always in the hands of a man. So would you be inclined to consider people as resources or money as resources? That is a personal question everyone will have to answer for themselves. But in doing so, remember this – people create money, money does not create people.

People are extraordinary resources, but having said that, it depends on how we see them. Advice from people can save you several thousands just as no advice from them can also cost you an awful lot. Until we begin to see that the absence of the right people in our lives can be potentially costly to us, and also that those in our lives are gold mines, we cannot begin to comprehend that we are potentially wealthier than we imagine. Do not get me wrong here. I am not advocating that besides people, physical money is not needed. Far from it; that is naïve thinking. We live in a world where as they say "money makes the world go round." Money indeed does get the world spinning. And indeed many things answer to money.

The biggest problem I have seen believers struggle with when it comes to them getting access to the resources they need to progress their vision is the mentality or notions they carry. And this is the notion they mainly carry: "I need to find money" to do this or do that. Why do we always think we have to GO and FIND the money? And some do go a long way to "find" the money—a very long way in some cases. But beloved, before God formed Adam, He made all the needed provision for him in Eden. The trees to provide shade, the vegetables and fruits to provide nourishment, the rivers to provide fish and a place to bathe, and the animals to provide him meat for food, shoes if he needed them, and fur to ward off the cold. They were all right there in the garden. **Right there in the garden**! Adam merely had to go and place a demand because he had dominion in the garden.

I ask this question regularly: Which of us on deciding to leave our child alone at home (if you can) will not leave food in the kitchen and let the child know where the food is before leaving home? Now, in the case where the child is too young to get its own food, would you not leave them at home with a nanny or an older sibling? Let me take the questioning a little further. Wouldn't you leave this nanny or older sibling with food maybe cooked? Why then do we believe that if we who are humans can think so well of our children, God in His infinite wisdom will actually place us in our Eden and in so doing place the resources we need to do well outside of Eden?

The sooner we quit thinking about God as some irresponsible, uncaring, unfeeling, and unreasonable parent, the sooner we will recognize that He has made provision for us WHEREVER He has placed us. I once watched a wise young man in my church build a successful shipping business from the ground up because he identified two sisters in the church who supported and helped him set up without much cost to him (I am not saying go out there and start taking advantage of people). One of the sisters was a business development and IT expert, and the other was an accountant and business adviser. It took them just two months to help him set up, and when they walked away his business was up and running. His resources were right there in the same church, right where God placed him. Yours may also be in the church, or perhaps amongst your family or work colleagues or circle of friends – these are all parts of your Eden.

A contradictory story to the one above is that of another young man who wanted to set up an export business, and he was telling me the big plans he had and how he intended to make it huge once he got his resources together. I kept listening. He was talking to me all the while but never bothered to ask me what I did for a living. I am a chartered certified accountant with specialisations in audit, accounting, business set-ups, and internal control systems. I had very good relationships with the two sisters mentioned earlier, and of course I also knew the first man who now owned freighting business.

Now, you tell me—if he had considered people as his resources, would his focus have been on finding money (physical cash) or rather on finding people around him who could help pull his business from the ground up? I have another question – if this last man had believed that whatever resources he needed to succeed in life were placed by God in his Eden, would he be looking outside for such resources? Stop looking at the ceiling! The answer isn't there!

If you can believe that the resources you need are nearby, your access will not be restricted in what you can achieve, but first you need to believe that God is kind, wise, considerate, thoughtful, and caring enough *not* to put you in your Eden and locate your resources outside of Eden. God is that kind. Even when it comes to money, there is always money around us. Believe me, money does not float around by itself. Money will always be in the hands of men and women. And you will be pleasantly surprised that the money you need to fulfil your dreams is in the hands of someone right by you. Maybe your neighbour, maybe your colleague, maybe your family or even a friend. It is always going to be right there with you as it was with Adam in the garden. It will always be right there.

Look at Jesus when He was born. Right there in the manger wise men from the East brought Him gold, frankincense, and myrrh. God didn't have to make Him or His parents go all the way to the East. Right there in the manger the costs of His upbringing and commencement of His ministry was paid for. Right there in the manger!

At other times the resource we need to bring a vision to fulfilment is in our own bosom, but we often don't consider it as a resource because of its size. Here is what I have to say to you. God does not look at sizes. Lift whatever you have before God and say, "Lord, I lift this up to You that You will touch it and breathe Your abundance unto it. I believe that what you have blessed will become infinite." And walk in faith, using the little that you have blessed. That little, I tell you, will never run out.

The Bible tells the wonderful story of Jesus feeding the thousands in John 6: 1-15 (AMP).

"AFTER THIS, Jesus went to the farther side of the Sea of Galilee—that is, the Sea of Tiberias. And a great crowd was following Him because they had seen the signs (miracles) which He [continually] performed upon those who were sick. And Jesus walked up the mountainside and sat down there with His disciples. Now the Passover, the feast of the Jews, was approaching. Jesus looked up then, and seeing that a vast multitude was coming toward Him, He said to Philip, Where are we to buy bread, so that all these people may eat? But He said this to prove (test) him, for He well knew what He was about to do.

Philip answered Him, Two hundred pennies' (forty dollars) worth of bread is not enough that everyone may receive even a little. Another of His disciples, Andrew, Simon Peter's brother, said to Him, **There is a little boy here**, **who has [with him] five barley loaves, and two small fish**; *but what are they among so many people? Jesus said, Make all the people recline (sit down). Now the ground (a pasture) was covered with thick grass at the spot, so the men threw themselves down, about 5,000 in number.* **Jesus took the loaves, and when He had given thanks**, *He distributed to the disciples and the disciples to the reclining people; so also [He did] with the fish, as much as they wanted. When they had all had enough, He said to His disciples, Gather up now the fragments (the broken pieces that are left over), so that nothing may be lost and wasted. So accordingly they gathered them up and they filled twelve [small hand] baskets with fragments left over by those who had eaten from the five barley loaves. When the people saw the sign (miracle) that Jesus had performed, they began saying, Surely and beyond a doubt this is the Prophet Who is to come into the world! Then Jesus, knowing that they meant to come and seize Him that they might make Him king, withdrew again to the hillside by Himself alone."*

Philip's position is the position we all are inclined to take. On seeing the sheer size of the crowd that needed feeding (i.e. the size of the vision or dream) he quickly worked out in monetary terms how much it would likely cost to feed the five thousand, and then his first inclination was to think "oh dear, we have to GO and find some more money." The truth however was that as soon as he started thinking in terms of the money, his mind could only go as far as the two hundred dollars or pounds sterling they had in the ministerial account. In other words, his mind was only able to stretch as far as the money available. Money is finite. The largest amount you can imagine is the furthest your mind will go in terms of achieving it. Andrew on the other hand caught half of the revelation when he said—and I love this—"there is a little boy here."

The revelation Andrew caught, was to identify that what they needed was right there with them. It was right there. But he killed the second part of the revelation by looking down on the size of the food available as compared to the task it was meant to accomplish. He compared the two fish and five loaves (seven in all) available in number to the five thousand in number (and anybody could work the math). It was impossible to match seven with five thousand. Jesus, however, did not allow Himself (His faith, His Spirit, or His soul) to be contaminated by Philip's monetary thinking not by the comparative arithmetical reasoning of Andrew. After all was said, the first thing Jesus uttered was "make all the people sit down." He never asked Philip "where can we get the remaining money to buy the quantity of food needed?" Nor did He ask Andrew how many more fish and loaves would compare favourably with the five thousand people. He said, "Make all the people sit down."

Jesus knew three things, two of which we have already discussed. When He brushed aside the fretting of Philip and Andrew, took the bread, and blessed it, He was confirming those three things He knew:

1. That whatever vision God gives to you He has made available the resources to accomplish it.

2. Every resource needed to accomplish your dreams and vision, God has placed in your Eden, not outside of it. Wherever God has located you with your goals, your resource to accomplish it is also right there with you.

3. If you look at the size of the available resource, you will diminish the accomplishment hidden in it. It is what the seed in the fruit is capable of that matters and not the fruit itself. God in His sovereignty placed five little loaves and two little fish in the hands of a little boy, and he was standing there all by his little self. Jesus saw beyond the size of the loaves, beyond the size of the fish, and beyond the size of the little boy and his little hands. Jesus saw

what God could do. He saw the multiplying power of God in thanksgiving and blessing.

Here is a mystery: The miracle of multiplying whatever resource you have available into proportions that become enough to facilitate your dream and vision is hidden in the **blessing** and **thanksgiving**. I'll start with thanksgiving first. The Bible says in Hebrews 11:1 (AMP) about faith:

> *"NOW FAITH is the assurance (**the confirmation**, the title deed) **of the things [we] hope for**, being **the proof of things we do not see** and **the conviction of their reality** [faith perceiving as real fact what **is** not revealed to the senses]."*

Now please follow me carefully here! We created beings in our limitation can only work life forward. By that I mean we only live life in the forward direction. When we live from 12 p.m. to 12:30 p.m. we cannot go back to 12 p.m. right? God on the other hand has no limitation with time and space. He can enter back and forth into yesterday, today, and tomorrow (Hebrews 13:8 and 2 Peter 3:8). Everything that has ever become a "reality" for man was before then a "hope" or an "expectation." In other words hope is our yesterday, reality becomes our today, and tomorrow is our confirmation. Confirmation is the point where we can boldly say, "I used to want Z and I got it at point W."

Let me show you why thanksgiving is the greatest act of faith by asking you a question. When do you naturally give thanks for something? Let's be very honest here – is it before or after you get what you want? It is after you get it right? Sure it is – it is a natural act to show gratitude (or even genuinely feel the need for it) after you have been satisfied with a reason to be grateful. There is a natural instinct in us to be grateful after our desire is satisfied. Now giving thanks is an act of tangibility right? It's tangible because your mouth utters it and your ear hears it. If it is uttered to a person, that person hears it. If it is uttered to God, God hears it. Sometimes we may even buy a card or make dinner or put an offering in the offertory basket to make our heartfelt thanksgiving more tangible. But the point still remains that giving thanks is tangible because it has a physically expressive component to it. Can you imagine someone buying you a very nice car for your birthday, you see the person the next day, and you merely look them straight in the eye and say loudly in your mind "THANK YOU! THANK YOU SO MUCH! I really liked the car!" Um, I don't think they can hear you! That's very intangible. The point I am making is that true giving of thanks is indeed a tangible act, and when you give thanks you do so because something tangible has materialised. This is the natural order of things:

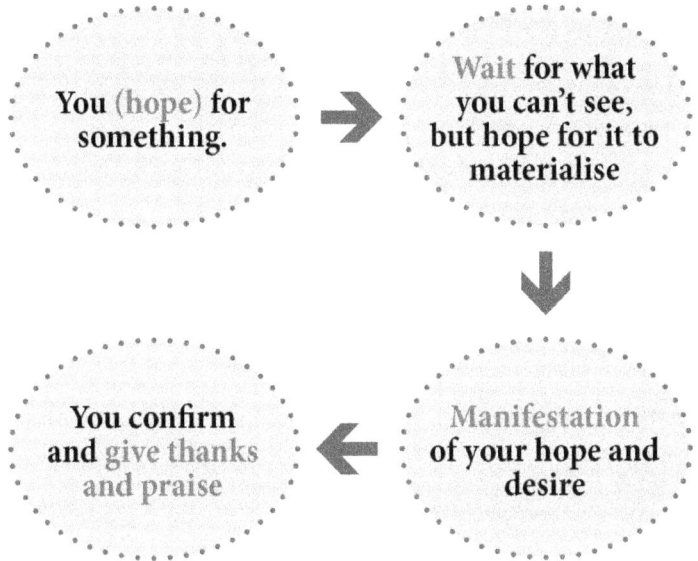

By the very definition of "faith" all four elements must take place. But more often than not we believe that faith is only exercised when we are in the waiting period. The beauty of this process is that faith's definition does not state which should come first, neither does it say which part of the process you must do and which part God must do. It simply says what the components are. Here then is the revelation – hope for whatever you'll hope for (as long as it is not of a wicked, evil, or selfish intention), then give thanks and praise to God Almighty for the manifestation of your hopes and expectations, and finally ask Him to work on the remaining two middle parts of the process. I challenge you to see whether your waiting time for things you have expected do not shorten drastically. This, my friend, is the working of faith.

Let me break down those two steps, the step of hoping and the step of giving thanks. I have come to realise that many Christians, even at the hoping stage, *doubt* whether what they are hoping for is moral or in the will of God. Well, let me help you there. Yes, we all know that whatever we pray and hope for should be in the will of God, and therefore most people resign to the point where they simply say "if it is the will of God, then let it happen". Hmmm. Really? But what is your will? What the Bible means by that is that your will *must* be in tune with the will of God concerning your life. I am sure someone will say, "Ah! Now he has really complicated it." No I haven't. Follow me here very carefully.

God created man in His own likeness, not partly in His likeness, but fully, which means that every nature of Him including His will is also imbedded in you. Intrinsically speaking, the will of God is already in you. God could not however exist as flesh on the earth to exercise His will (because He is Spirit), hence the reason He created you to be on earth IN HIS FULL LIKENESS to exercise His very nature on earth – including His will. So then you should come to the realisation that you are here on earth as a full representation of God, encompassing His will, His joy, His peace, His riches, His judgment, His glory, etc.

Before the fall of man, Adam and Eve were in such perfect synchrony with God that they didn't have to think twice whether or not the will they exercised was in tune with God's will, it just was. After the fall however that synchrony was altered. Man couldn't see clearly through the link he had with God in Eden, but God's will and every part of Him that was in you in that Adamic beginning is restored to synchrony with Him once you accept Jesus Christ as your Lord and Saviour and the Holy Spirit dwells in you.

The question to be answered then is how do you know that your will (which from the very beginning was the will of God in you on earth) is still in tune with that of God? That's a very good question. Understand the attributes of God. He is faithful, pure, wealthy, strong, just, beautiful, righteous, loving, forgiving, orderly, not an author of confusion, and so on. **If all the known outcomes and possible outcomes** of whatever you are hoping or praying or believing God for, will increase any one or more of the attributes, whether to you or to someone else, then indeed your hopes and expectations and desires are in tune with the will of God.

I frequently hear young people who want to marry say, "Well, if it is the will of God for me to marry, then let His will be done." Yes, His will shall be done when you realise that His will has to be exercised through yours. God is not physically here on earth, but His will is in you and it is you who has to exercise it. A "will" is not a dormant activity. It has to be exercised. God does not go back on His Word. When He created man He gave man dominion over the earth and He never took back nor will He ever take back that dominion from man. God is a respecter of order, including the order He Himself has established. That is why He will always need man's involvement here on earth to make things happen. He gave man dominion over the earth – He will *not* jump that queue and just do His own thing on earth without man's involvement.

Anyway, back to the example of those who want to marry – in saying if it is God's will for me to marry then I will, what you are effectively doing is saying to the devil "I do not have a will to exercise." You are effectively denouncing the will of God already embedded in you. What I rather suggest you do is say OK, I desire to marry. And then ask yourself what would be the outcome if you got married – your soul would be glad and so would that of your spouse. Is one of the attributes of God joy? Yes! So joy would increase in the earth. Maybe in marrying you will be fruitful – is one of the attributes of God fruitfulness? Yes it is, so the fruitfulness or increase of "God's image" here on earth will multiply (since we were created in God's image, believers multiplying also multiplies the image of God on the earth).

If on the other hand you were considering taking over someone else's spouse for yourself, then you should consider that the outcome of your desire will be pain, heartbreak, and loss for that person whose spouse you are about to take. The question is does God's attribute include pain, heartbreak, confusion and loss? By this action therefore you will be increasing pain, heartbreak, confusion and loss in the earth. Effectively, you are out of tune with God's will. You know what to do from that point onwards. Need I say more?

So next time your will is desirous of something, don't just sit there and say if it is the will of God. Instead identify what the possible outcomes of your desires are and match those outcomes against the attributes of God. Will the outcomes be increasing or decreasing the attributes of God in the earth?

Now, unto the second part of exercising faith—giving of thanks. Have you ever wondered whether angels in heaven have needs? I have. Do you realise that a greater part of their duty is to continually bow before God and worship Him, bless His name and praise Him? (yes, they also guard and minister to the children of God, carry out prayer assignments, and wage war against fallen angels). I think it is fair to say that more than ninety per cent of prayers from us Christians is focused on asking, not thanking and blessing God. No wonder ninety per cent of the time we are in need. Consider how The angels in heaven spend a hundred per cent of their time blessing, worshiping and thanking God, and throughout the Bible we have never once heard of an angel being needful. And yet they are meant to minister to us. Serve us. I wouldn't be surprised if so many angels have asked themselves, "What is wrong with these human beings that we are meant to serve, huh? They are always in need, and yet we who serve them are never in need. Ah! Why?" I really wouldn't be that surprised. Think about it. Do you think that it was mere coincidence David spent years of his life writing the Psalms and singing them in worship to God and became the greatest King of Israel? Do you think it was by a stroke of luck that Abraham was always blessing the name of God by building Altars and memorials and making Sacrifices to God and became the father of Israel and a friend to God?

Look at the <u>diagram</u> above and analyse it very carefully again. Don't you think God also knows that it is a justified progression for anyone to receive "thanks" after fulfilling someone's desire or need? Of course He knows. Now answer these questions to yourself in all genuineness:

- Do you think God has ever and will ever put Himself in a position of being indebted to any man or woman here on earth?
- Do you believe God knows that you'll naturally be more inclined to give thanks to Him for His goodness toward you?
- Do you then also think that God is a cheat?

I am glad you answered these questions in all genuineness of heart and not purely for the fear of God because here lies the truth: If you genuinely give thanks to God for something you are *yet* to receive from Him, God will *not* take, inhabit, and enjoy your worship of Him and your praise to Him and *not* manifest the reason or purpose for which you are praising Him. God dwells in tangible praise. And your praises and thanksgiving to God for an expectation is made tangible when God brings to fulfilment the reason for the praise. Now you know how to exercise your faith.

Have a desire. Pray to God about it, genuinely worship and bless God for the fulfilment of your desire— and watch God bring it all to pass, quickly. For many years we may have gone ahead of God in the faith walk, and in going ahead we have chosen the hard parts of the faith process and left the easy parts to God. In fact most of us have come to think that "we" must carry out ALL the steps of the faith process. Well, except you allow God, He is not going to interfere with you when you are exercising your will on earth.

Many of us know the story of how Abraham became the father of faith because he agreed to offer up Isaac as a sacrifice to God in Genesis 22. Brace yourself for another side of the story. Abraham, when he was asked by Isaac where the lamb for the sacrifice was, said to the lad "God will provide." After this stage, he had a choice. He could have chosen "to wait" for the lamb to be "manifested" by God before proceeding to "give thanks" for the lamb. But guess what he did? He skipped the waiting and manifestation parts of the faith cycle and jumped to the giving of thanks bit. How? Well, this was not the first time Abraham had had to make a sacrifice. Genesis 22:9-10 (NKJV) says:

> *"Then they came to the place of which God had told him. And Abraham built an altar there and placed the wood in order; and he bound Isaac his son and laid him on the altar, upon the wood. And Abraham **stretched out his hand**...."*

In actual fact, what the translators of the original text didn't properly corroborate here was that Abraham gave thanks by stretching his hand with the knife in his hand. It was the traditional custom of the time that no sacrifice on an altar to God would be made without thanking God for the lamb of the sacrifice. So you see, he carefully chose which parts of the faith cycle to exercise by his will and which parts to leave to God. Here is what Abraham knew – God could not receive a thanksgiving for providing the lamb without actually providing "the lamb."

Now let's talk about the blessing, the other component needed to multiply the little resources you have available to become enough to fulfil your destiny walk. The first component is thanksgiving, which we just talked about; now, blessings. The Oxford dictionary's definition of blessing is "God's favour and protection" or "a prayer asking for divine favour and protection." Please hold on to that definition. The two main Hebrew verbs for blessing are *barak* and *ashar*.

Now I want you to capture a very fascinating trend in the Bible. Anytime a "blessing of God" was decreed over or asked to come upon a thing or a person, it was ALWAYS followed with a statement or evidence of a corresponding "increase," or we would read some verses or chapters down how the previously blessed item or person "increased or multiplied." It's all in the blessing, and consistently too.

God Was Ready for You a Long Time Ago

- In Genesis 1:28 God blessed "them" (Adam and Eve) and said "multiply" (*rabah*). How profound. Notice that the word "bless" here was used as a verb, meaning it was an action God carried out towards Adam and Eve, and right after that He commanded them to "multiply." God is a God of order and sovereignty. Maybe you should ask yourself – God could have just commanded Adam and Eve to multiply. Why did He have to bless them first before directing them to multiply? I'll wait – tell me the answer when you are done thinking!

- In John 6:11 Jesus blessed the fish and loaves of bread, and they were multiplied enough to feed five thousand men besides women and children. Again, understand that Jesus was the Son of God. He had undeniable authority and power; even the devil during his temptation of Christ confessed he knew that Jesus could turn stones into bread. Was Jesus therefore trying to teach His disciples and us something about blessing when He chose to bless the bread and fish instead of just commanding the food to be multiplied? Why couldn't He just ask Philip to run to the seaside, catch some fish, and get some gold out of its mouth as He did with Peter in Mathew 17:27? After all the multitude of five thousand that needed feeding were gathered by the **seaside** (where there would have been a lot more fish). Don't worry, I have a lot of patience to wait; tell me the answer when you are done thinking!

- 1 Chronicles 4:10 (NKJV) reads, *"And Jabez called on the God of Israel saying, 'Oh, that **You would bless me indeed, and enlarge my territory**, that Your hand would be with me, and that You would keep me from evil, that I may not cause pain!' So God granted him what he requested."* It is worth noting that unlike the New Age generation, the patriarchs and men of old did not just get up and pray. They meditated on what to pray, how to pray, and when to pray it – they didn't just get up and pray. If you are honest to yourself, you'll admit the way you pray is far different from the prayers you read in the Bible uttered by the great men of old. It is not by random coincidence that Jabez, in his prayer, asked God to "bless" him first, and only after that did he ask for "the enlargement and expansion." Think about it! Why did he ask for the blessing first? Couldn't he have just prayed and asked for an enlarged territory?

- In Genesis 27:26-29 Isaac blessed Jacob. Three chapters later, in Genesis 30:43, it is made evident *"thus the man (Jacob) became exceedingly prosperous."* I find something very fascinating here. If you read the entirety of Genesis 27, Esau, upon finding out that the blessing had been pronounced on Jacob, reacted this way in Genesis 27:34 (NKJV): *"When Esau heard the words of his father, he cried with an **exceedingly great and bitter cry**, and said to his father, 'Bless me—me also, O my father!'"* He was more than angry. Now this is where the intrigue comes; he does NOT immediately chase after Isaac to deal with him, but he rather kneels before his father and asks *"bless me—me also, O my father!"* And his father indeed blesses him. In Genesis 33 when Esau finally meets up with Jacob – he was almost equally as blessed as Jacob – this is what he says to Jacob in verse 9 (NKJV): *"But Esau said, 'I have enough, my brother; keep what you have for yourself.'"* Isn't it amazing that in Esau's extreme anger he considered that the more important thing was to still get some "blessing" from his father before chasing after Jacob? The blessing must have meant so much to him that it enabled him to quench his anger long enough to approach daddy Isaac for it. Think about it – in his utter bitterness he still falls on his knees to Isaac and says, **"Bless me—me also, O my father."**

- In Genesis 17:17-20 Abraham, knowing that Ishmael is not his chosen heir and *cannot* thus bless him with his own lips (talk about him understanding the order of God!) but instead asks God to do so. God on the other hand yields to Abraham's request and "blesses" Ishmael in 17:20 saying, *"And as for Ishmael, I have heard you. Behold, **I have blessed him**, and will make him fruitful, **and will multiply him exceedingly**. He shall beget twelve princes, **and I will make him a great nation**."* Did you notice that God blesses him first and then subsequently speaks of exceeding multiplication and fruitfulness? Do you think it is mere coincidence the Islamic race is "exceedingly" wealthy? Ishmael is their father – **God blessed him**, and let me add, because Abraham asked God to. It's all about the blessing; believe me, it is.

- In Genesis 12:1-3 God first blesses Abram then subsequently adds that those who bless you shall also be blessed. In other words, those who cause you to increase in any way will themselves also increase – it is God who spoke this, not a man; there is therefore no chance, not even one in a gazillion, that He will go back on this offer. Why then do you think after all is said and done that America can hardly turn its back against Israel? No! She would rather bless Israel and her people and continue to be "a blessed America." America today remains the number one country that aids Israel – that's why she'll never go down. I could go on and on about the blessing of God and the increases that come with it. Of a necessity, blessings must flow from an authority higher than the person wishing it. So it is perfectly in order to ask blessings from God and from the authority figure in one's life, be it your parents or spiritual head. There are however two main things about blessings and their release that one should be aware of.

Firstly, God is a respecter of authority and a staunch respecter of order – He does not jump queues and does not practice confusion. God in His wisdom respects the fact that there are certain blessings He can and will release on you and others that people in authority in your life must release over you. Take these three scenarios: Abram through Sarai's maid begot Ishmael. Traditionally, a servant, their physical body, and their possessions belonged to their master (that's why Abram said to Sarai in Genesis 16:6, *"Your maidservant is in your hands, do to her as you rightfully please"* [paraphrased].

Thus, apart from the fact that Hagar was not legally Abram's wife, Hagar's whole life and everything that came out of her life as a servant was owned by Sarai. In other words, on those two counts Ishmael could *not* fall fully under the authority of Abram – that's the reason why Abram could not release a blessing over Ishmael. In that particular instance he asked God to bless Ishmael. Read Genesis 17 again and see for yourself. It was God who blessed Ishmael.

The second scenario is this: Abraham later blessed Isaac, his real heir, and the blessing on Isaac was later transferred as a blessing to Jacob and Esau (we already talked about this). Order was being put in place and authority was being respected.

Esau knew that his blessing was deposited in his father Isaac and that God respected that order and authority, hence he could not simply walk up to God and say, "Listen, God, that guy you gave me as a brother has taken my blessing so I need You to fix me a new set of blessings, OK!" He could easily have done that but he didn't. Think about it. In all his vicious anger towards Jacob he still found a way to convince his father to "release a blessing over him." I sometimes feel sorry for people who think they can be at loggerheads with the authorities in their lives and still easily make it through in life.

The final scenario I want to share with you is Jabez (1 Chronicles 4), who prayed directly to God that a blessing be released over him. Well, he was not contradicting order or surpassing authority. He did not have a father. The name Jabez was given him by his mother. Traditionally at the time and even now, a woman could not name a child unless the father was not alive or he had forsaken his fatherhood rights over the child. And again traditionally (and this is still the case) where family is concerned, authority remains in the hands of the fathers.

Now it is worth making clear that having authority figures in one's life is *not* entirely by blood or birth relationship. It can also be by election. The disciples of Jesus elected by their own will to submit to Jesus, and by that He blessed them. Elisha by election served under Elijah and received a double portion of his spirit as a blessing. Joshua was blessed by Moses, and yet he was not the blood son of Moses. So whether you have authority figures in your life by birth or by election, I suggest you run to them the moment you finish reading this chapter, and with a sweet smelling offering in your hands **ask them to bless you** with every blessing within them that is worthy of receiving. This is wisdom, and if you are wise you will do this.

I emigrated from Ghana and had been living in the UK for quite a while when my eyes were opened to the power of parental blessings by my prophet and teacher, Rev. Dr. James Osborn Nanjo in 2007 and 2008. I remember very well I didn't hesitate one bit – I was on the next available flight back home, laid a good offering at the feet of both my parents, and asked them to bless me. And bless me they did. Oh, how I thank them. Bless me indeed they did, from the depths of their hearts, and I can tell you one thing for sure – my life changed from that point on, and it's been all joy and expansion.

Go get your blessings if you are reading this. My two personal pieces of advice to you are these. Firstly, if you have parents who you may not be on good terms with, find a way of sorting that mess out because the truth is—and I don't care what you think about this – a big part of your blessing and expansion in life is wrapped up and placed in their (guess where) tongue. Secondly, if you have a spiritual authority over your life, strive to do the same with them. I remember quite vividly going to see my spiritual father, Dr. Nanjo, "properly". He blessed me greatly.

And in blessing me he prophesied over my life. And day by day I see a manifestation of every such prophecy. - nothing has been missing since. I bless God for Him.

The problem with most Christians is that they expect to receive everything for free. But the truth we fail to realise is this: Just as in the physical world there is such a thing as a "medium of exchange," in the realm of the spirit, spiritual things can also be transacted. Question is, what are you transacting your spiritual business with? There is something about the human soul that when it is in a state of joy, fulfilment, or excitement, it oozes out more than it naturally would. Fact! Isaac, in Genesis 27:4 (NKJV) said:

> *"And make me savoury food, **such as I love**, and bring it to me that I may eat, that my soul may bless you before I die."*

Isaac understood that when his soul was excited from enjoying what he loved, his blessings over Esau (as he originally intended) would ooze out freely and bountifully. Now you know how to trade and receive an "overflowing" blessing. Again I say to you go get your blessing, whether by relation, by election, or directly from God – go get your blessing.

I love what I am about to say to you right now. Here it goes. The blessing that comes from heaven is eternal, but most importantly it shares the greatest characteristic of its source – it is limitless, it is without boundaries. Take a balloon and the air that fills it up; which of these two is more abundant than the other? Take a bucket and the water used to fill it up; which one of the two is more limitless? The more limitless things, for example the air, can make a limited thing like a balloon, suddenly expand to so many times more than its original size. In fact the balloon is filled with the limitlessness of the air to the degree that its skin can stretch.

Jesus, when He lifted the loaves of bread and fish to heaven and blessed it, essentially asked the food to be filled with the limitlessness of heaven, and because heaven had more than enough to feed the entire population of the world from the beginning of creation to the day God brings on the apocalypse, the only limit to the expansion of those few loaves and fish was the number of people available to eat it. If I were you, I'd be lifting some things to the heavens right now. Wow! We almost drowned in all that sweet spirited sea! Now the second thing about the blessing is this: A man cannot bless you with what he does not have. You don't even have to read this from the Bible to know it. Apostle Peter said to the beggar at the beautiful gates in Acts 3:6 (NKJV), "*Silver and gold **I do not have,** but **what I do have I give you**: In the name of Jesus Christ of Nazareth, rise up and walk.*"

Indeed Peter could have blessed him with silver and gold if he had any at the time, but the crippled man would have finished spending it and be right back at his spot the very next day. Peter knew exactly what he was carrying, and he intentionally wanted to establish that fact—the fact that he was about to give the cripple exactly what he carried: life. And that's exactly what he gave the cripple – life to his crippled body. Something all the people he had been begging from all these years could not give him. But of course they couldn't give him life – they didn't have it. In 2 Kings 2 Elisha by election served Elijah, and by that very election and service he was in the position to be blessed by Elijah. At the point of Elijah's departure, when he asked Elisha what he wanted, what he was in fact doing was asking Elisha this profound question: "What blessing do you know me to possess that you want me to bless you with?" If Elisha, throughout his service to Elijah, did not recognize that Elijah had a strong anointing of God upon his life, then believe you me there is no way he would have received that anointing and more from Elijah. Remember this – a man cannot bless you with what he does not have. Elisha's response to Elijah was twofold, and this is what he asked for in 2 Kings 2:9 (NKJV): *"Please let **a double portion** of **your spirit** be upon me."*

One part of that answer shows us that Elisha did recognize Elijah as possessing an anointed spirit from God. Now look at this: Elijah responded saying, *"You have asked a hard thing. Nevertheless, if you see me when I am taken from you, it shall be so for you; but if not, it shall not be so."* It was indeed a hard thing because Elisha was asking Elijah for an anointing, which was more than what Elijah himself knew he was carrying. A man cannot give what he does not have. Elijah had the anointing, yes, but Elisha was asking for twice what he had. But the Bible tells us that Elisha indeed got the double anointing he asked for. The question is how did that happen? I'll explain, not by my own thoughts, but by the kind revelation of the Almighty, to whom I am eternally grateful.

When Elijah made the comment quoted above, what he was in fact doing was making a petition to heaven—a petition that when the heavens opened up to receive him, the extra portion of his anointing be released upon Elisha. Elijah understood that once the heavens were opened up, a double transaction could occur at once – angels could both ascend with him via the chariots and descend to Elisha with a second portion of anointing. He understood the events that happened to Jacob in Genesis 28 when Jacob slept with a rock for his pillow and caught a vision of angels descending and ascending. Elijah understood that he himself had just one spirit, one anointing. And this anointing is what he left for Elisha in his mantle. The second anointing that was needed to make it a "double anointing" had to come from heaven, hence the reason Elijah said to Elisha, "….*nevertheless if you see me taken away from you….*"

Right after that the Bible clearly tells us that Elijah was taken up to heaven by a whirlwind, and Elisha saw it. Like Jacob, Elisha saw heaven, and in that very instance he also experienced angels ascending with his master Elijah and descending with his second portion of anointing. A man cannot bless you with what he does not have.

I had an interesting experience when I was about to get married. My wife and I came up against a strong opposition when we both decided we wanted to get married. We decided to go back to Ghana to have the ceremony, considering that both of our parents were back home. Due to very strange occurrences, circumstances did not permit my spiritual father, Dr. James Nanjo (I bless God Almighty for his life), to travel with us even though he had prepared to bless our marriage.

My wife-to-be and I had to make alternative arrangements in finding an officiating pastor for the ceremony, and it was in the process of discussing these alternatives that my spiritual father made me see a very profound angle to this decision process. He said to me the very thing I say to you now: "No man can bless you with what he does not have." And he was right. If a man has not been blessed with a successful and solid marriage, what then can he bless another with? But taking this a step further, it is more than marriage. It is applicable to every area you need the blessing for. If the people of authority in your life do not have the blessing you seek to receive, if they themselves have not been blessed with it, then by all means you will not be jumping the queue when you go to God and say, "Bless me, O God, with Your blessing of...."

In conclusion, look around you; the resources you need to achieve your vision or build your dreams are all around you. It may be small like the little lad, or it may even look ridiculously tiny compared to the vision and destiny that God has placed in your heart, just like the two fish and five loaves looked ridiculously tiny compared to the thousands to be fed. But remember there is a way out – two ways in fact. Firstly, let your thanksgiving rise up to heaven for the resources God has already endowed you with, no matter how small. This is true faith in action. And finally, seek, find, and provoke the blessing upon what you have, whether it is directly from God or from someone in authority in your life in whom God has already deposited such a blessing. And remember – no man can give you what he does not have, but if he doesn't, God does.

PRAYER POINTS:

1. Thank God and worship Him for the resources you have available in the form of people, money, etc., no matter how small they are. Thank Him that He has placed these resources in your hands to further the cause of your destiny.

2. Now ask the **blessings** of God upon these resources and pray that as the blessings pour forth, the resources may be multiplied and become regenerating and plentiful enough to fund all your needs and desires here on earth to the glory of God.

3. Pray and ask God for the leading of the Holy Spirit to help you locate the people in your life with which He has deposited some of your blessings, so that you can honour them and release your blessings.

4. If there are authority figures in your life with whom you are not on good terms, pray God to release your heart and satanic veils over your eyes to see and recognize that these persons have a role to play in your destiny's advancement, and also ask for the wisdom to mend all such relationships.

5. Pray and ask God to help you trust Him completely that you may exercise true faith through thanksgiving and worship.

6. Pray and ask the Holy Spirit to lead you daily to walk in the will of God and to also identify that the Holy Spirit's dwelling in you is effectively the will of God being represented because He only speaks to us what God asks Him to say. John 16:13 (NKJV): *"However, when He, the Spirit of truth, has come, He will guide you into all truth; for He will not speak on His own authority, but whatever He hears He will speak."*

7. Thank God for being so kind to equip your "Eden" with all the resources you will ever need to be a shining light in the earth to the glory of His holy name.

4

Lord! Where Did You put the Diamonds?

In conducting my own research, I have come to the conclusion that about ninety per cent of us who work do not excel at what we do. I am talking about "excel" to mean being the absolute best at what you do and totally, totally loving to do it. In fact, this has a profound connection to what some of you may have read in the past – that about ten per cent of the world's population controls ninety per cent of the world's wealth. I think that's a very diplomatic way of putting it so that we continue to be blinded from the truth. What is really being intended for our understanding is that ten per cent of the world's population controls the remaining ninety per cent.

If you still don't understand that, let me break It down a step further: ten per cent of the world's population that excels at what they do controls the lives of the remaining ninety per cent who do not excel at what they do. I guess now it's all getting clearer huh? Well, as bitter as it sounds, that is the truth. Solomon in Proverbs 22:29 (NKJV) paints the picture in a very beautiful way: ***"Do you see a man who excels in his work? He will stand before kings; he will not stand before unknown men."*** (The phrase "unknown men" comes from the Hebrew *chashok* meaning "insignificant and obscure.") See! Let's be very honest here. Think about anyone who you think excels at something, anything – take Lionel Messi who excels at soccer, or Bill Gates who excels at information technology. Then also take someone who has not excelled at what they do. Now I want you to ask yourself which of these two sets of people is likely to be invited to meet up with other great men. Good. You might on the surface think the men and women who excel at what they do have a greater chance of coming into the presence of great men and women because they are rich, but that's exactly where I'll ask you to STOP! In fact, no, they will not stand or come into the presence of kings and great men because they are rich; rather they would do so for one and only one reason – they excel at what they do.

Here is another way to look at it – coming into the presence of great men and kings because of one's excelling at something effectively means being approved by great men and kings. That's the fact. Great men and kings will only bring into their presence what they approve as worthy and excellent. Let me explain something to you. Every great person, king or queen, has a great following (it's the only reason why they are great). This following of people usually believe that the great person must have done something right to get to the level he/she is at, and therefore it is not a coincidence that they too, in aspiring to be great, will attempt to do the things that the great person does, approve the things he/she approves, despise the things he/she despises, dress like them, speak like them, and the list goes on – all in a bid to be great like them.

Now can you imagine a man who excels at what he does being approved by any of these great people? That man will automatically be approved by the followers of the great man too, and in so doing he/she also becomes great. How did it all start? He excelled at what he does.

This is the wisdom (of course) in Solomon's words *"do you see a man who excels **in his work**?"* Please read over that text seven times slowly, each time digesting the underlined text. That's the revelation right there. A man who excels does not excel at what somebody else does but rather at what he does. He excels at **his** work, not what his father asked him to do. He excels at **his** work, not what his family does. He excels at **his** work, not what his teacher told him to become.

The two big questions which the ninety per cent of us keep running away from are these: What do you do now? Are you doing what can be considered as YOUR Work? If you ask me, I think you should put this book down after reading this chapter and dwell on those two questions for about a week or so, because answering them will be the key to changing your entire life from mediocrity to excellence and from insignificance to kingship.

It took me twenty plus years to ask and answer those questions. I remember back in the lower classes of my secondary school years, I used to do so well in the arts subjects. When it came to selecting a specialisation, however, I opted for the sciences. Why? Because my dad was an exceptional building technologist, my uncle (his younger brother) was a highway and urban planning engineer—and it goes on. There was no way I was going to become anything less. That was my idea of excellence – to be exactly like those who were in my eyes already excellent. To me, being anything other than that meant bringing myself to a "lesser" repute.

In other scenarios, I have had friends who opted to study the sciences because their dad wanted them to become doctors or engineers. Yes, some of us may excel to some degree at what we are doing now, but the truth is that what we are doing is not what we should be doing. It is NOT our work.

I have, by the grace of God alone, come to know three paths to employ in determining what the gem in you really is, in other words what you should excel at in order to stand before kings and great men. If you are thinking to read through all three of them and select one to apply then you've got it wrong from the start. All three must align to each other. They MUST.

Path 1: Searching Within Thyself:

In Proverbs 4:26-27 (NKJV), wisdom speaks to us as follows:

*"Ponder the **path** of your feet, and let all your ways be established. Do not turn to the right or the left…."*

I am led by the Spirit of God to make you understand this text very well and why there really is the need to search deep within yourself to find **your work** [the only work you should excel at], so please do stay close to me.

If you have ever walked on or seen a ***pathway*** before, whether in a park or through a jungle or even through the lawn in your garden, you will not have difficulty understanding that a path is created by repeatedly walking along a particular line. *Repeatedly* is the word. A path cannot be created if you don't repeatedly walk along that line. Now, the most important reason for creating a path is so you will be able to reach a certain destination, hence a path is created from point A to point B. Once that path is created, it will bring a lot of things into the picture.

1. It will ensure that you consistently reach a certain destination.

2. It will determine the timeframe within which you reach that particular destination and the destinations beyond it.

3. That path becomes a reference point on your daily walk and can easily let you know whether or not you are getting lost, walking astray, or deviating. This third point is the reason why verse 27 says, "*Do not turn to the right or the left….*"

Having now considered the three effects above that a path brings to your journey in life, is it any surprise that verse 26 admonishes us to "***ponder** the **path** of [our] feet*"? In other words, think deeply about the path you are creating because once that path is created, everything else in your life is established based upon it. Your marriage, how you raise your children, your fellowship with the Holy Spirit, your relationship with other saints, whether you can afford to go on holidays, whether you can afford to buy a house or even sponsor the work of God's kingdom – it will all be established based on the path your feet create. That is why I repeat: think deeply about it.

Now here is the meat on the bone you just chewed: Do you recognize that the particular career, job, employment, self-employment, calling, or profession you are engaged in is what takes more than fifty per cent of your days and weeks and months and years? Now tell me that is not substantial and I'll stop right here! Think about it. Consider the amount of time you spend at work. If life therefore is a journey and destiny's fulfilment is the point you want to get to, then it presupposes that your "path" is the over fifty per cent of your days that you spend on work and the thirty per cent that you spend on sleep. The question however is this – have you thought deeply and thoroughly about these paths? Is this the path that will ensure that:

1. you do in fact reach your destination (that's assuming you know it)

2. you do indeed reach your destination in time (remember you are not going to be here forever and that time and tide wait for no man)

3. you never wander away from your destiny?

I am not saying that work and diligence are bad; on the contrary, that is the theme of this book. What I am asking you is whether you are walking the right path. The Bible is asking us to THINK CAREFULLY. THINK about the path you are plying.

Phew! You can breathe in now. I'm really thrilled by all of this. If you go further down to Proverbs 16:9 (NKJV), the good Word of God makes a profound statement: *"A man's heart plans his way, but the LORD directs his steps."*

What this scripture is telling us is that we have a part to play in letting God bless us. It says here very clearly that *you* have to plan the way. In other words, ponder it deeply, pray about it, ponder it again even more deeply, and then choose it. And when you are done, God in His all-knowing power, because His eyes are in every place of the earth, will *direct* your feet. God is happy for you to create the path, but He will tell you when walking on that path, "Son, put your feet here because over there is a nail that could pierce your feet," or He would say to you, "Daughter, place your first step to the right and the third one also to the right because on the left there is a cobra crossing the path."

What other collaboration do you want? You draw the path and God teaches your feet how to be most effective in walking it. The Bible never said God will plan your path and then also direct your feet to walk on it; that's spoon-feeding – it said He will direct your steps on that path. Your steps! Your feet! Your steps! NOT the path on which He directs the feet to walk. I am known to tell people that every human being, but more so every child of God, is pretty much like a self-contained package that God has dropped on the earth. That's the way I see it. In him or her is everything he or she is ever going to need to be an ambassador of God here on earth. Look at the American embassies all over the world in various countries – they stand out. The business (or **work**) at those embassies and consulates is conducted in such a way that it reflects the power, authority, superiority, dynamism, and wealth of America. This is the case because the ambassadors are fully equipped when being sent on such missions, and I mean fully equipped.

Now here are two things I want you to catch from that. Firstly, these embassies and the resident ambassadors could not have reflected America's power, authority, superiority, dynamism, and wealth if America itself as a nation did not possess all of this. So ask yourself are you exhibiting every level of awe and glory exhibited by God, from whom you were made and whom you were sent to represent here on earth? If not, are you then accusing God of not having equipped you adequately? Just asking!

Secondly, one of the reasons why America is perceived all over the world as being all the things I listed above is because her ambassadors and embassies portray the same (powerful, superior, dynamic, and wealthy). It's not so difficult then for people all over the world to conclude that if America's representatives are so outstanding, then the land of America itself must be very outstanding. You can't blame them.

The question worth asking ourselves is this: As God's ambassadors here on earth, what image are we painting of God? Does our life show that He is weak, poor, powerless, lacking innovation, inferior and most of all without direction? Just asking! Now getting practical, there are questions we should be answering that would help us search within ourselves, which is something we don't usually do consciously enough. Although I could find different ways of helping you ask the searching questions, I find it effective to pose them as follows:

- What do I do best with the greatest ease?
- What am I naturally good at that nobody else does as well as the way I do it?

- What is it that I can do easily, over and over again, and yet still be excited about doing?

It's tempting to take the easy route out of the park and say to yourself "I don't think I am really good at anything." That is a lie of the devil from the pit of hell. You are either finding an excuse not to think or you are trying to tell God, "Hey, big man! I think You forgot to add something unique to this lump of clay when You created it, you know?" And that in itself is also a lie. As long as there is "the breath of God in you," there is also divine uniqueness in you.

Think, think, and think! Take about thirty minutes to an hour for three days (works best in the very early hours of the morning when your mind is fresh from rest) and retreat into seclusion. Find a way and a place not to be disturbed, pray the Holy Spirit to lead you into all truth about yourself, ask the questions above, and then proceed to meditate and dwell on answering them truthfully and genuinely for the next thirty to sixty minutes. Think. Have a notebook handy beside you on each of these days and write down what you think is in you that you do more uniquely than others.

There's definitely something in you that you feel uniquely outstanding about. It doesn't matter how ridiculous it is. It may be as ridiculous as you being excellent at taking off cobwebs or even fixing broken brooms – that's not the focus; the focus is that you list down in a very genuine way what you feel uniquely best at doing better than a lot of people. There's got to be something. It should include everything you feel you are good at as well as personal attributes you are easily disposed to (oral communication skills, confident, interpersonal, deep thinking, etc).

I am not asking you to necessarily come up with something that any man or woman on earth has never done before; far from it. This is personal. Forget about what your friends and family have told you, forget about what you have seen other people do and to which you may have whispered to yourself "Ha! I can do better than that." No! This is you looking very, very deep inside yourself for answers. It is not about puffing up yourself with respect to how multi-talented you are; rather it's about being spot on, being true, and being real.

Don't worry if you don't find an answer in three days. All you have to do is simply extend the days you need to get an answer from within yourself. It doesn't mean you are dumb or stupid, it simply means everybody is different. It may be that you haven't been used to thinking about yourself this way, and thus you may need some adjusting to get into the swing of it. Whatever it is, make sure you go through it and come up with something. I am not asking you to come up with a list. In fact if you carry out the exercise properly, you should come up with no more than three items on the list. One or two is perfectly fine too as long as you do not stop after the first day.

The reasoning behind doing this over three days is to ensure that there is some consistency in your internal thinking process.

If on the first day you ask yourself the above questions and you come up with a list of three, on the second day a totally different list of four, and on the third day a totally different list of two, then there's got to be something wrong with the approach or you have merely repeated some of the items on the list, but that's alright. Even though you take each day separately on its own and shut out the thoughts of all the other days, still there will be a common thread in the answers you come up with.

I implore you not to look down on the simplicity of the entire process. The complexities of God's abilities are most often than not wrapped up in the absurdity and simplicity of His divine directions. Don't ignore this one. In 1 Corinthians 1:27 (NKJV) the Bible says:

> *"But God has chosen the foolish things of the world to put to shame the wise, and God has chosen the weak things of the world to put to shame the things which are mighty."*

Now that you have this list, fold it up, tuck it in an envelope, label it "The First Path," and stash it away in a secret place.

Path 2: What Does the World Say About You:

I am sure you have just looked at the subheading above, and the first thing you may have said to yourself is "He's having a laugh at me! The world doesn't know me." WRONG! The world is the few people around you that you know and who know you. That is the world. The way you interact with them, think about them, and react to them is exactly what the billions of people in what you call the "world" will be expecting from you.

There is an interesting concept in business marketing I want us to explore. In the business world companies exist and remain in existence to serve people. It doesn't matter whether they make profits or not, they exist because of people. If they make profits, they do so because they are doing something that people need them to do and continue doing. If it is a not-for-profit organisation, then it means it is continually getting money just to spend because those giving the money believe that these not-for-profit organisations are serving the needs of people. Either way it's all about people.

The companies that succeed are those that listen to the people they serve. Those that do even better are those that listen to both the people they serve and those who could potentially become their customers. In other words, they listen to those they are currently serving and those they can potentially serve. They listen. To a businessman or better still to a company, one customer or one potential customer is still a pot of gold. Businessmen understand that one person's need is a replica of several other people's needs and that satisfying one customer is effectively satisfying ten other potential customers. There is something in business called "strategic focus" and it basically means:

1. A company asks itself what it is that it does better than anyone else, and after that

2. The company asks its customers and potential customers what it is that the customers feel, know, or believe is the reason why they keep coming back to that company (in other words, the company wants to know what its customers think it is good at)

And based on the outcome of these two, the company focuses on doing what it does best, thus satisfying the needs of its customers better and even winning more. It is biblical. Mathew 16:13-17 (NKJV) reads as follows:

> "When Jesus came into the region of Caesarea Philippi, He asked His disciples, saying, **"Who do men say that I am?"** So they said, "Some say John the Baptist, some Elijah, and others Jeremiah or one of the prophets." He said to them, "But who do you say that I am?" Simon Peter answered and said, "You are the Christ, the Son of the living God." Jesus answered and said to him, "Blessed are you, Simon Bar-Jonah, for flesh and blood has not revealed this to you, but My Father who is in heaven."

Jesus was a very knowledgeable man. And His knowledge was both supernatural (by the Spirit of God in Him) and natural (by

His education in the Torah and Jewish laws). He could have asked His disciples "do the people say I am Elijah?" and they would have answered "yes." And He could have asked again "do you think I am Adam?" and they would have answered "no" or "yes." Notice when He asked who people said He was, He was referring to people outside His circle of disciples, and He got more variety of answers than when He asked His own disciples who they thought He was. Some (the non-disciples) said Jesus was Elijah, John the Baptist, or one of the prophets, for example Moses.

People who have not gotten the opportunity to get close to you in any way will conclude who they perceive you to be OR what they perceive you to be capable of being to them. Their judgements will be based on one or all of the following:

- what they can see or experience about you physically (some may have based their judgment on the miracle of physical food Jesus made available using the five loaves and two fish, hence their quick reference to Him as Moses, who was the leader of the Israelites when they ate manna in the wilderness after leaving Egypt)

- what they need you, want you, or would like you to be (some may have said Jesus was Elijah because they needed a prophet in that season, somebody who could cause the rains to stop and bring the Roman leadership to its knees in that era). Indirectly, they were expressing a need in their lives. A need they believe Jesus would be the right candidate for.

When He asked His own disciples who they thought He was, the text says clearly only Simon Peter answered. All the others were quiet. Isn't that fascinating? A minute or two earlier they were all chatting away about the different variations of who people thought Jesus was, and when He asked what they themselves thought, there was silence – because they didn't think Jesus was any of those people. Otherwise it would have been so easy to repeat and say "oh we think You are John the Baptist or Elijah or one of the old prophets just as the people have said," but they were quiet except Peter.

Why? They knew all too well Jesus was carrying a greater Spirit than what any of the old patriarchs carried, and that's exactly what their dilemma was. A big dilemma for that matter because on the one hand they didn't need anyone to tell them that Jesus was next to God if not God Himself on earth. They had heard Him speak in public and in private to them; they knew the depth of His wisdom and insight was not human. They saw His miracles. They knew who He was. He was the Son of God.

The dilemma arose because, on the other hand, their Jewish teachings and culture did not permit them to even assume, let alone believe, that God could be present in human form or that there could be any messenger greater than any of the patriarchs of old. No! There could not have been one much greater than them. There must not be. It is therefore not surprising that people outside of the Twelve did not hesitate in limiting Jesus to be equal to one of the old prophets. Not more. Jesus' commendation of Peter therefore was for him (Peter) choosing to overcome the teachings and traditions of men (flesh and blood) and believing in the Spirit of God he saw at work in Jesus. Flesh and blood (the Jewish teachings and traditions) would have taught him (revealed to him) that God could not come down and live amongst men in the flesh. Flesh and blood would have taught him that none could be greater than the prophets of old.

This is the second practical step to identifying what you should become excellent at. You'll need to find ten people who know you very well. Try to make it a mixture of people who know you from work, school, church, home, or wherever, and try to avoid picking a list of people who you know will tell you what you want them to tell you. Call them up or meet with them and tell them you are making a big move in your life, and part of the move means you need people to give you an honest, blunt, and truthful assessment on what they are convinced you are good at.

This assessment should include everything they feel you are good at as well as personal attributes that you are easily disposed to (oral communication skills, confident, interpersonal, deep thinking, etc). Ask them to put aside all the niceness and be as honest as possible. Since they have known you or worked with you, ask them what they genuinely think you are good at or that you do very well. Let them understand they are under no obligation to say you are good at anything. If you are not, they should just say. You'll not take it as an offence.

Whatever they say, write it down—every single one of them—and thank them genuinely for helping you out. They have done your destiny a big favour, and I trust if you follow this book through to the end, you'll one day come back and thank them for their honesty.

Another way I have found this path to work well is to resign to a place of quietness and try to remember clearly some of the times in the past when people have told you that you were good at something and really meant it. If you can't remember any of these instances, that's fine, just concentrate on the original plan of gathering the information from ten people who currently know you well.

Whatever the method you have chosen to use, write down everything the ten people have said to you and those you have been able to remember from the past. As in the first instance, put this list in an envelope, label it "The Second Path," seal the envelope, and hide it together with the first envelope.

Path 3 – Location! Location! Location!

This is a topic that should be a whole book by itself but which I'm going to try to condense as much as I can. There are two fundamental truths I want us to establish before we set out (both I am sure you already know anyway). One, God does not do anything in a vacuum; in other words, everything He permits, everything He fashions, everything He guides you to do, already has a purposed link to a future end. Most times the point in the future to which God links His actions in your life today are so far away that you may not understand why He is doing what He is doing today – He sees tomorrow, a year in advance, five years, ten years, twenty years in advance; in fact He sees it all before you are even formed in the womb as clearly as He can see this very minute unfold. He is omnipresent. Every point in the past, present, and future is before Him as presently as the words in this book are before your eyes.

So the bottom line is that God does everything for a reason and that all His works in your life in the past, in the present, and in the future are linked. The second point I want to remind you of before we jet off is this: God gave you a will. He knows you have that will and He respects that will. If it wasn't the case, He would have forced everyone to be born again instead of granting salvation to anyone exercising His will to "come" to Christ and "accept" Him as Lord and Saviour. To *come* and to *accept* are all doing verbs, and you have to have a will in order to "do" them.

Because God will not work against our will, He "leads" us. How much of that leading we get depends on how much access we give Him into our lives or how much of our will we submit to His will. I'll strongly recommend the latter though. And the only reason why I suggest that to you, which you already know, is so that He exercise His will on your behalf considering that he knows everything about the past, the present, and the future. Tell me if you wouldn't be seen as a fearful person if you knew everything about the past, the present, and the future!

We have managed to establish that everything the Lord is doing in your life today has the future in mind. It also follows without much reasoning then that everything He has been doing, and everywhere He has led your feet to in the past, was to equip you for today. So I ask you today, do you know where God has been leading you in the last couple of years? And here is the biting point: If you understand clearly "what" God has been doing in your life to date and "where" He has been leading your feet (and I don't mean physical feet) to date, you will be in the most critical position to figure out "what you were being equipped to do today."

So again I ask you, what has God been doing in your life and where has He been leading your feet? Where has He been positioning you? I think I prefer this last question more because of the word *positioning*. Living in England, I have been used to watching a property show on TV called *Location, Location, Location*, and the title of the program carried the entire philosophy of the real estate industry it was featuring, and that is that the location of the property determines to a large degree its value. So, in like manner, the position **you have allowed God** to strategically place you in, up until yesterday, is exactly so that today you can be ready to decide your perfected path. But before then a question remains to be answered: Where has God been positioning you?

Is it a particular word or action or direction He has been whispering to you to take for the past couple of years? Don't you think there is a reason He hasn't relented? Is it a particular ministry He has impressed upon you to follow and remain faithful to all these years? Why do you think it's been a waste of time to have followed that ministry? Why haven't you rather asked yourself what God is positioning you to learn from that ministry? Is it the location you keep finding yourself in? Is it how you have always wanted to leave Manchester for London, but God has always ended up giving you a genuine reason to remain in Manchester? Or that you have always meant to leave Virginia for Washington, and God has always found you a reason at the last minute for why you shouldn't leave Virginia? Could Manchester or Virginia be a strategic positioning for your destiny? Is it the kind of jobs you keep finding yourself in or a particular task your superiors have kept asking you to do for the past God knows how many years?

Before you start saying "I hate my job" and moaning about "my boss keeps asking me to do the same thing I have been doing for the past seven years," ask yourself, "Has God been positioning me for something greater? Was there something He wanted me to learn in all of this so that I can better understand what my chosen path is and hence become the best at it?"

In Exodus 2, the story of Moses begins. From then on it tells us how Moses was hid in water, how he ended up in the house of Pharaoh, how he was educated in the palace by the very best magicians, philosophers, linguists, diplomats, mathematicians, military generals, and astrologers, how he was chucked out into the wilderness to die, how he became a shepherd serving the priest of Median, Jethro—and on and on. That was God positioning Moses for His greatest role on earth – to lead Israel out of Egypt. He was positioned in water at birth, and his name even had a derivation from water because he was going to have to deal with the Red Sea. He was positioned to become a well-educated prince in the palace of Pharaoh because he was going to go back to the same palace and speak the same diplomatic languages that Pharaoh and his strong men could understand.

The Bible says in Acts 7:22:

*"And Moses was **learned in all** the wisdom of the Egyptians, and was **mighty in words** and deeds."*

It was all about positioning when he was thrown out of Pharaoh's palace into the wilderness to die because he was going to eventually lead the children of Israel right through the same wilderness. He was positioned to be a son-in-law to "a priest" because he himself needed the priesthood ordination to go before God on behalf of the children of Israel. And you bet it was all about positioning when he had to serve as a shepherd of goats and sheep and ewes because he had to shepherd Israel, he had to learn how to use his rod, he had to learn how to protect his flock and provide for it. It was indeed all about positioning.

Think again, where and how has God been positioning you? Get a clean sheet of paper and start writing. Be prayerful about it; ask the Spirit of God to take you back to the years behind and open your eyes to revelation on why you were where you were in the past. Now label this write-up as "The Third Path."

When you are well settled after reading this chapter, I need you to pull out envelopes 1, 2, and 3 and open the contents. Look through the lists in envelopes 1 and 2 and write down the thoughts and ideas and truths that have come out most similar on both of them. Keep filtering down until you come to a list of three at the most. Call this new list "A" (the things you are best at doing). Now I want you to match list "A" with the list of God's positioning on list number 3. If you do this right and in all honesty, you will realize that a great part of God's positioning on list number 3 will point you towards your suitability for one item on list "A"(two at the most). If you are convinced in your spirit about what you have arrived at, I suggest you fast and pray about it immediately.

I heard you saying "fast and pray again?" Well, I don't know how much value you place on your destiny, but this is "a path" or better still "the path" your destiny will be walking on for a long time to come, and it makes perfect sense to put some investment into it. There is no feeling greater than the joy, the peace, and the fulfilment you get from knowing you have found your path. Oh believe me, you will feel just how wonderful it is. Congratulations, you have arrived safely at you destination.

Glory be to God, the most high God of Israel. I am truly excited for you. I really am.

As a child growing up, there was a proverb that always caught my excitement and it goes like this: "Birds of a feather flock together." It literally means that birds identify what company they should be in by looking at the feathers of the other birds around them. This is very true. Of course it doesn't take a genius to figure that eagles do not fly with ducks although they are all classified as "birds," nor will ostriches walk with vultures, even though they are all classified as "birds." The truth, my dear friend, is that this phenomenon of association is applicable to all creation. It is the way God intended it – hence the reason why in Genesis 1, the Bible repeats over and over the phrases "after their own kind" or "according to their own kind." When He created the sea animals, He did so after their own kind; when He followed with the birds of the air the Bible repeats "after their own kind"; and so on and so on. God established the law of association by identity from creation, and so it will remain for eternity.

Earlier on we learnt that people who come before kings are people who have found ***"their way"*** or ***"their work"*** or ***"their gem"*** (theirs, not someone else's), and in finding their way they have become perfected and diligent in those ways. Proverbs 25:2 (NKJV) says:

> *"It is the glory of God to conceal a matter, but the glory of kings is to search out a matter."*

In other words, working, making an effort, searching, and finding the gem that God has placed inside of you promotes you into "kingship". It is your success in finding the hidden gem in you that gives you kingship. A king cannot rule except he has a kingdom and finding the gem in you equates to finding your kingdom. God has deposited a kingdom in everybody, so Jesus was not lying when he said in Luke 17:21, *"For indeed, the kingdom of God is within you."* And it is because of this kingship and your consistency in working at preserving, polishing, and making better this discovered gem in you that establishes your kingship.

Once you have arrived at that kingship point, then by God's law of identity association you too will come into the presences of those "after your kind" – kings. Indeed, just like birds, kings identify better with kings. Great men identify with great men. Excellent women identify with excellent women. **Great people are people who are always searching, and the greatest thing anyone can find is their self.** What makes you think great men will associate with you if you haven't found anything? Well, what have you found? It is finding yourself that describes you to them as "one after their own kind" or "one according to their own kind."

A very popular scripture you may know is Romans 8:19-22 (NKJV):

> *For the earnest expectation of the creation eagerly waits for the revealing of the sons of God. For the creation was*

subjected to futility, not willingly, but because of Him who subjected it in hope; because the creation itself also will be delivered from the bondage of corruption into the glorious liberty of the children of God. For we know that the whole creation groans and labours with birth pangs together until now.

The Farles' Free online dictionary defines *revelation* as "a dramatic disclosure of something not previously known." You see, here is a truth you may not have known about this scripture. In other well-loved translations it says *"all creation groans for the manifestation of the sons of God."* Why does creation groan? Because she has a need, a need that she has desired for so long and yet has not been satisfied with because those in whom the solution to that need is hidden have refused to "reveal" the solution that God has hidden in them – their gem.

In Psalm 98:1-2 we are made to understand more clearly why God needs us to be revealed. Our revelation, our discovery of the gems in us, is His salvation to the world. In other words, the solution God has provided to the groaning world is this – **we should be revealed**. So henceforth understand this, that the gem in you is God's solution to the needs of the world. God has already created demand for the gem He has hidden in you. You are here on earth carrying God's answer to a particular need of the entire creation. If that need remains unsatisfied, if the whole of creation continues blaming God for not satisfying such a need in the world – it is your fault. It is your fault that you haven't searched to discover what God has placed in you; it is your fault that you have hijacked God's supply to creation's demand; it is your fault that creation does not believe God when God answers them and says, "But I already sent you the solution to the problem you had...I deposited it as a gem in Michael, in James, in Harry, in Olivia, in Angela, in Mary, in Joel..."

I repeat, God's solution for a specific need of all humanity is deposited in you as a gem. If creation and all its inhabitants are still groaning because a particular need has not been satisfied yet, it is because the solution, the gem in you, is still lying dormant – unfound and unrevealed. It is a very grave matter. Think very carefully about NOT making the effort to discover your God-deposited gem.

In conclusion, what do you know yourself to possess? What and who do people say you are? Where has God positioned you? Jesus was a "vine tree" in nature and a "carpenter" by profession. Why do you think He had the ability to take raw plain wood such as unlearned fishermen and build them into magnificent arks like great carpenters do? Excellent Christian arks in which He deposited His anointing! His death on a **tree** was no coincidence. He was a vine tree; ending His life hanging from a tree at Calvary was not a coincidence. The nails? He had worked with as a carpenter's son. Paul was a scholar, a prolific writer, and an exceptional legal brain before he found Christ. Why do you think he wrote the most profound books of the New Testament and put forward the most un-contestable defence regarding Jewish and Roman Citizenship? What do you have? What does the world believe you have? Where have you been positioned? Will you let the world continue groaning in expectation because you have chosen to divert and hoard the supplies God has promised and delivered to the world? Think about these things – they are indeed worthy of your indulgence. Think about these things.

You have God's answer to the world inside of you. What are you doing with it?

PRAYER POINTS:

1. Thank God and worship Him for the honour He has done you by placing a gem in you (He placed in you a solution to a need in the world).

2. Ask God to forgive you for not having worked at discovering the gem He deposited in you earlier and for causing His creation to groan all this while.

3. Ask the Holy Spirit to lead you into the knowledge of finding the gem God has deposited in you. The Bible says in John 16:13, *"However, when He, the Spirit of truth, has come, He will guide you into all truth; for He will not speak on His own authority, but whatever He hears He will speak...."*

4. Ask God to touch your heart and the hearts of the people you'll be employing in search of your hidden gem with truth, honesty, and the fear of the Lord.

5. Pray that as God opens your eyes to the hidden gems in you His own Spirit will preserve such a gem in you for His glory. Ask Him to give you a new spirit of obedience to deploy your gem for the solution God intended it to be.

6. Once you have found that precious path/gem, commit it to God and ask Him to bless it, that it may be preserved and multiplied for His glory. Ask Him to direct your steps on the true path that He has helped you to find.

7. Bless the name of the LORD and ask Him to give you speed and strength that you may become diligent at your work or your way so that your destiny will come before kings. Remember, you were originally created as a *king*, a *royal priesthood*.

5

Even as Your Soul Prospers —Is He Serious?

It's the soul first, my fellow heirs in Christ Jesus. If you do it any other way, it won't work.

So what happens after you have discovered your gem? My experience tells me this is the part of the process that requires the greatest level of focus and discipline. It's the part that is easy to throw off and say to yourself, "Oh, whatever! I don't need all this; I think I'm doing just fine." If that is what you resolve, then I can justifiably conclude two things – one, that you are either lazy and you are trying to rationalize the need NOT to "diligently excel at what you do" as the Bible emphasises in Proverbs 22:29 (NKJV), or better still you are pure selfish, not only to yourself and your fellow mankind but also to God. Why to God you may ask? I'll answer by asking you a question also. Do you genuinely and honestly think that God placed a gem in you just for you? Do you think the world will stop groaning for your manifestation simply because you choose not to be "diligent" or "excel" in using your gem, your talent, your hidden gold?

It's okay if you choose to rationalize that neither of these arguments applies to you, that's absolutely fine. I would just like to remind you however that we are all like the servants to whom the master gave talents of gold and departed away in Mathew 25:14-30 (please read this). When the master, Jesus, comes back, we will be asked to account for every talent He endued us with – the gem in you being the biggest.

So back to the question, what do you do after you have discovered your path, your gem, your talent? Well, every mineral diamond that is dug from the earth does not attain its highest value until it is cut and polished. It's the cutting and polishing that makes it glittery, attractive, and desirable. Jesus, even though He had the Spirit of God upon and in Him whilst He was here on earth, yet in His human vessel secluded Himself between His twelfth year and His thirties before resurfacing. Do you think in that timeframe He was merely eating His mother's food and sleeping in His father's house? No! He was polishing, polishing, polishing. It's the reason why when He came out, He shone. So bright, in fact, that He could not be resisted.

Take His disciples for example; Jesus was God here on earth. Don't you think He had enough power to simply take His disciples to the top of a mountain, lift His eyes to heaven, and call on His Father to supernaturally make them super apostles, ready for the ministry? Yes He could but no He didn't. He took His time and polished them. For three years He polished and polished and polished them all. So here is the first thing you ought to do – polish the diamond you just discovered within yourself. And I mean polish. Yes you have a unique ability, yes it is peculiar to you alone and none else, and yes nobody does it like you do. And the list goes on.

But hold on! This is planet earth and things are done slightly different here than they are in your mind. So please go ahead and start doing some polish work. The fact that you have a raw diamond doesn't automatically mean everybody is dying to see it in an exhibition. What would they be looking for, the mud and dust on it? Nay. On the contrary, if you are a peculiar diamond that has been very well shaped and thoroughly polished, it makes the difference between whether you go on display in a gallery for the whole world to see or remain in a pouch, tucked away somewhere. The word is "polish thyself."

You need to understand that what you have inside you needs to be presented in a "certain way" for the world to notice, and in their noticing for the glory of God in you to be revealed. That's the way to bring honour to your Father in heaven above. Learning what this "certain way" is, is what the polishing process is all about. It's about understanding how the medium through which you express your gem works.

So say for example you discover your ability to speak and hold people's attention, and the path you have chosen to best express that is by being a TV presenter. That's all well and good, but you have to learn the way to cast news, you have to learn the things you can and cannot say on TV, you even have to learn what to wear and how to behave, how to smile, how to operate the basic equipment, the etiquette of TV presenting. Or maybe study journalism or professional presentation skills. No producer in the world, no matter how much raw talent you've got, is going to pick you up and stick you in front of a TV camera. Believe me it won't happen even if an angel should appear to them in their production room and tell them to do so. They won't, no sir, no madam. And you sit down and cry, "Nobody is noticing my talents." Well, your talent is NOT glittering enough to catch their attention. What are you going to do about it? Get it polished. If I was standing on a pulpit (Lord, help me) I'd probably ask you to turn to the person sitting next to you and tell them "go polish your precious gems, pal."

See, I have reckoned thoughtfully about the popular saying "all that glitters is not gold." I figured the reason why this popular warning came into being was because as soon as something glitters, it catches the eye irrespective of whether it is copper or glass or diamond. If it shines, everybody wants to have a feel of it. But becoming a Christian made me understand this very well. Ecclesiastes 11:7 says, *"Light is sweet, and it pleases the eyes to see the sun."*

Light is responsible for glitter. Where there is no light, you will see no glitter. In fact you would not be able to see the most polished diamond in a room that is pitch dark. So although it has been very well polished, its glitter becomes useless in the absence of light. That is not the sad case with the believer. See, in the case of the believer, God plants the light in you. It is internalised; 2 Samuel 22:29 says, *"You are my lamp, O LORD; the LORD turns my darkness into light."*

God's whole idea of depositing both a gem and His light in you is so that the glitter of the gem He deposited in you will never be hidden by darkness because there's always going to be light inside of you to keep that glory glittering. If He thought your gem's glitter could be sustained without the light, He wouldn't have created the light in you. The way I see it, God knew all too well that you would at some point need to polish the gem in you, and when that happened, you would need the light to keep it shining. Matthew 5:16 says, *"In the same way, let your light shine before men, that they may see **your good deeds** and praise your Father in heaven."*

God is a perfect God, He is an established God. The things that are wrought by His hands are things that stand forever. He knew that if the continual glittering of your polished gem were to rely on the light in the world, then its glitter wouldn't last for long – because the light of the world gets very dark most times. So what does He do? Places inside you a custom-built light to ensure that the gem He's deposited in you, and which you have polished up, continues to shine. Matthew 5:14 says, *"You are the light of the world. A city on a hill cannot be hidden."*

This is what the book of 3 John 1:2 (NKJV) says:

> *"Beloved, I pray that you may prosper in all things and be in health, just as your soul prospers."*

Surely this is a very popular scripture amongst Christians. My intention in applying it is to show you another face of it. The first thing I want us to notice about this scripture is this – it links your prosperity in ALL things to the prosperity of your soul, meaning that in anything or indeed in everything you wish to prosper, the first point of call should be the prosperity of your soul concerning that thing. It ends up by saying *"just as your soul prospers,"* meaning that so long as your soul continues to prosper in regard to a particular thing, you'll continue to prosper and be in good health regarding that thing. So if your soul prospers in the area of marriage, then in the physical realm you'll prosper in marriage. If your soul prospers in the area of wealth and riches, then in the physical also you will become wealthy and rich, and so on and so on.

Now let us take a look at making your soul prosper. In this book however we are limiting ourselves to prospering your soul with regards to your newly found gem – your path in life, the path in which you ought to excel.

The most common Hebrew word for "prosper" is *tsalach* (tsaw-lakh'). It means "to advance, or to make progress." The Greek word for "prosper" is *euodoo* (yoo-od-o'-o), which also means "to have a successful journey." Finally, one of the English definitions of the word *prosper* is "to grow or to increase." Putting it all together, to prosper here therefore means "to have a successful journey of growth and increase."

Now, we bear in mind that your prosperity in something is dependent on your prosperity in your soul concerning such a thing. The question then is how does your soul prosper, or to replace the word *prosper* with its meaning, "How does your soul have a successful journey of growth and increase in order for your newly discovered gem to also have a successful journey of increasing?"

The usual word for "soul" in the Old Testament is the Hebrew word transliterated by the letters *nephesh*. We find one example in Genesis 2:7: *"The Lord God formed man of the dust of the ground, and breathed into his nostrils the breath of life; and man became a living soul [nephesh]."* The *nephesh* is the state of consciousness itself. In this connection, *nephesh* can be used in a general sense to stand for your seat of emotions and thinking.

Good. Now that we have a clearer understanding of the two core words, let's try to re-piece together the passage we read earlier in 3 John 1:2, which says: *"Beloved, I pray that you have a successful increase and growth in ALL things and be in health, just as your thinking and emotions in those things increases and grows."*

As you may have already noticed, this is not exceptionally different from our earlier conversation of polishing up on your raw gem that has now been discovered. Of if you choose not to call it a gem but rather a path, then the idea would not be to polish it but to tar it so that the tarred path becomes easy to ply and faster to walk on. From the above breakdown, it appears there are only two approaches to being successful in our newfound path – increasing in learning (thinking) and excitement (emotions) about it. I will not go much into the increasing in learning bit as it is very obvious. If you want to be the best at something, you grow your thinking in that regard. It's a fundamental law, and I explained that earlier even in the case of Jesus and His disciples.

When you learn more about something, your thinking and mindset about such a thing also changes. Your mental confidence and decision making with regards to such a thing become sharper. You see, it was not mere babbling when the great apostle emphasised in Romans 12:2, *"And do not be conformed to this world, but be transformed by the renewing of your mind, that you may prove what is that good and acceptable and perfect will of God."*

In other words, your newfound path gets transformed from a raw path in the grass to a super highway that everyone wants to walk [drive?] on, by the renewing (learning) of your mind. Your newfound gem gets transformed from its raw and muddy state to a polished and highly glittery revelation of God's glory in you by the renewing (learning) of your mind.

The other aspect to ensure your prosperity in your new path is "emotional," and we will focus on your need to understand why your emotion regarding this new path (or gem) must be positive.

Let's not beat around the bush; if you are reading this book, you are most likely older than thirteen so you should know this

– haven't you ever noticed that you do better in the things that you are excited about as opposed to the things you feel miserable about? It's not a coincidence. It's your soul at work. Your soul is like a little rudder in that it directs the whole ship (you) in the direction you should go. Interestingly, the ship (you) is so dependent on this rudder that the ship cannot turn in its own direction outside the direction of the rudder. That's just the way God made it. Being excited in your soul about something is simply directing the rudder (and hence the entire ship) positively northward, and feeling angry, frustrated, unhappy (and all the negative emotions) is simply directing the compass (and hence the entire ship) negatively southward. So now you know, the more excited you are about your newfound path, the more excited you are about your gem, the more your life automatically gets aligned to make it succeed. It's your soul at work.

You have a choice here. And this is the one thing I love God so much for – that in all His giving, we've also been given an opportunity to make choices. Nobody has the right to blame God for not being successful in life. A case in point is that everyone who reads this book up to this point has a "choice" to either go back and take control of their gem, polish it, and reveal the glory of God to all creation (who have been groaning for it since the foundations of the earth) or to pack up the book under a stash and get back to their old selves. They have a choice to share their insight from this book and in so doing ensure that the glory of God deposited in their Christian sisters and brothers is also revealed. Or you can simply keep quiet and let the glory of God rot in those brothers and sisters. The choice is always yours.

In Genesis 27:2-4 (NKJV) we read about Isaac in the following:

> *"Then he said, 'Behold now, I am old. I do not know the day of my death. Now therefore, please take your weapons, your quiver and your bow, and go out to the field and hunt game for me. And make me savoury food, such as I love, and bring it to me that I may eat, that my soul may bless you before I die.'"*

What Isaac, a patriarch, understood that most of us don't by reading the passage just on the surface was that in eating savoury food of meat which he dearly loved, his soul was going to be excited, gladdened, and blissful, and when this happened the positivity of his soul was going to be highly charged and in the process excellent blessings released "from his soul" over Jacob (who by the way he thought was Esau). Again in Genesis 8:20-21 (AMP) we read:

> *"And Noah built an altar to the Lord and took of every clean [four-footed] animal and of every clean fowl or bird and offered burnt offerings on the altar. When the Lord smelled the pleasing odour [a scent of satisfaction to His heart], the Lord said to Himself, I will never again*

curse the ground because of man, for the imagination (the strong desire) of man's heart is evil and wicked from his youth; neither will I ever again smite and destroy every living thing, as I have done."

Notice that before the Lord made the decision (He said in His heart) not to destroy the earth with a flood again He was "pleased." Being pleased is an emotion, and what I want you to notice here is the marvellously positive result a positive emotion can bring to the entire world. I reckon it's about time you started getting very excited about your new path, your new vision, your new gem.

In Mark 14:33-34 (NKJV) we read:

"And He took Peter, James, and John with Him, and He began to be troubled and deeply distressed. Then He said to them, 'My soul is exceedingly sorrowful, even to death. Stay here and watch.'"

Jesus here experiences death in His soul first. He was still in a human vessel and felt the things that humans also feel, but the most important thing to notice is that He permitted death to be felt in His soul first. As a result His whole humanness was able to conform to the need for His death on the cross.

What you now feel or indeed what you permit yourself to feel concerning your path, concerning your gem, concerning your dreams, will by all means determine where that dream ends up, where that path leads to, whether to a successful growth and increase or death. It will determine whether that gem becomes manifested, becomes priceless, or goes back into its raw and muddy state. In computer terminology there is such a phrase as "what you see is what you get" (WYSIWYG). In our context, however, it may actually be of relevance to say *"What your soul feels is what your life gets" (WYSFIWYLG).*

I strongly feel led to add a powerful insight here. I used to be in your position, and I must confess it can be very difficult to feel excited about something you can't see. Here is the solution – create mental images and pictures of how perfectly you want your gem to turn out. Create images of it being a blessing to the world. Create images of it being so useful to humankind that they will bless God for your life. Create mental images. It is these images coupled with the excitement generated from them that will produce the manifestation.

Creating these mental pictures is exactly what is referred to in Proverbs 23:7, *"As a man thinks, so he is."* In other words, you will become what you continually think about. My practical advice to you is this – form mental images of how you want your gem to bring glory to God, and dwell on it day and night. Some may refer to this process as meditation. That's all well and good, but whatever you choose to call it, form mental pictures about your gem, dwell on them, and allow your soul to be excited about your gem, for surely What You See (in your mental images) and Feel in your soul Is What You Will Get (WYSFIWYWG).

Follow me closely here: I want you to pick any object in front of you, stare at it for a minute, then close your eyes and picture the same item in your mind. Good. Now I want you to close your eyes again and picture a bicycle in front of you. Any bicycle. That wasn't too difficult either was it? Good! Have you noticed that the ease with which your mind could **hold a picture** of something that is physically in front of you is the same ease with which it could **create a picture** of something that wasn't physically in front of you? That's the whole idea of calling into being those things that be not as though they were. Calling into being here refers to "calling into mind" the bicycle that was never physically in front of you as though it was indeed in front of you physically. You see, the mind cannot differentiate whether or not what you are calling into memory does exist physically.

What we tend to classify as reality are the things happening or appearing in the physical realm, which get registered on our mind and which we then accept as true and therefore as reality. But that is just one side of reality. The other side of reality which we often don't know or practice is this – to create and accept exciting images in our mind as real and true which the physical world around us is forced to accept and bring into manifestation because it is a reality in our mind. In the former scenario, the direction is from the physical to our mind, whereas in the latter the direction is from our mind to the physical. It's really a matter of choice whether you want the physical world around you to design and create a life for you to accept or whether you choose to design and create your own life for the physical world to build for you.

The law which forms the basis of what is called meditation in simple terms states that whatever exists in the physical exists in the mind and vice versa. Let me give you a very basic example. Car designers, before they come up with a new model, already have it in their mind. They would have seen the model over and over again till it becomes so real to them in their mind, and then it becomes real in the physical. It's the same with say a wedding for most women. They dwell on it, some of them from childhood till it becomes so real to them that when they finally see the physical wedding dress or flower arrangement or cake, they know without blinking if it matches the image they have created in their minds or not.

So here is the summary – create mental images of your gem and how you expect it to shine and be a blessing to many to the glory of God. Dwell on these images regularly with excitement in your soul until your gem becomes very real to you; then you will see a manifestation in the physical. You will have succeeded in calling into being those things that be not, as though they were.

Now I believe you have a good enough reason to not only polish up the gem God has deposited in you but also to form vivid images of its manifestation, be excited about it, and then see it come to realisation. Let your soul be enthused about it. Talk about it, dream about it, and finally it will materialize.

PRAYER POINTS:

1. Pray asking God to lead you in the process of polishing your gem, shining your talent, and plying your newfound path diligently until it serves the full purpose for which it was deposited in you.

2. Pray to God and ask that His light in you will continue to shine in order for the gem in you to be a light to the world.

3. Ask God for divine excitement in your soul concerning your gem, your talent, or your path.

4. Pray to God to give you the wisdom to form images about the manifestation of your gem, your path, etc., in line with His holy Word so that your manifestation doesn't instead become an offense.

5. Pray and ask God to grant you divine consistency in holding onto your godly images of the things that be not until they are fully manifested as though they were.

6. Ask God to lead you (by His Holy Spirit) to be a blessing to your fellow brothers and sisters by introducing them to the deep insights you have received in reading this book.

7. Finally thank God for everything you have learnt up to this point and His greatness that is waiting to be revealed in you soon.

6

5…4…3…2…1…
ACTION!

The greatest failure of any man is not equivalent to him trying something and not succeeding at it; the greatest failure is actually NOT doing anything at all, not acting at all, especially when you have what it takes to act – that is failure. An even greater failure is to know there is something in you that is for the benefit of the world and yet never utilizing it (hey, women… don't run away, there is the word "man" in "woman" too!).

Once you've figured out what you carry, do something with it, please. I am begging you. Please. The one reason that has contributed to the largest number of dreams not being fulfilled is this – the dreams were never acted upon. So the dreams remained dreams and that's exactly what they will be. Act now.

I know many of you reading this book may have heard this story, but for the sake of others let me repeat it here. A farmer found a newborn baby eagle that had been blown out of its nest in a storm. He took it to his wife and she tucked it under the welcoming wings of a mother hen. The eagle grew up with the brood of chicks thinking he was a chicken. A few weeks later a neighbour was startled to see the creature pecking and picking and scratching in the dust along with the other chickens. **He lifted it into the air, saying to it, "You are an eagle, you do not belong to the earth. You belong to the majesty and glory of the skies above. You need to flap your strong wings and fly away."** But it fluttered and squawked and jumped safely back onto the ground. The farmer laughed and said, "He's grown up like a chicken; he thinks he is a chicken; leave it alone. I think that's where it belongs – with the chickens."

The neighbour ignored the farmer and tried again. He carried the eagle up to the roof of the hut and threw him out into the air, but the eagle saw only the safe circle of his chicken siblings down on the ground below, so he flapped and scraped his way back to join them again. And the farmer and his children laughed fondly, for **they, without any doubt, accepted that the eagle was really a chicken even though it still had every feature and facet of an eagle**.

But the neighbour would not give up. Before dawn the next day, he travelled up into the mountains with the eagle. As the first rays of light began to pierce the sky, the man climbed onto the highest edge of a cliff. He held the eagle up to the rising sun and whispered, **"It's okay to try, but whatever you do, you must flap**

your wings. Fly, eagle, fly!" The eagle trembled as he looked into the light. The wind ruffled his feathers, and as the sky flooded with brilliant gold rays, his true nature asserted itself. **He lifted his wings and began to fly.**

I have intentionally highlighted certain parts of the above story only because I want you and me to relate to them in depth. This book, if you have read to this point, has (I hope) pretty much told you everything that the farmer's neighbour told the eagle. Yes, you may have walked around people who have not seen your potential or even helped you to identify what it is, but that is OK. Now you know it, now you have a dream; if this book has done nothing at all it has done this one thing – I am telling you today, here and now, you are an eagle, and I don't care where you are in your life right now. All I care about is letting you know that the sky is yours together with its limitless power – you have the life-creating breath of God in you, the very breath by which He created everything in the earth. You know you are more than what you think you are. You know you are more than what the earth has pushed you to be. You know you are a joint heir with Christ Jesus (Romans 8:17). Do you think God, in His absolute and exceeding greatness, will have sons and daughters as heirs who are weak? NO! God believes in you and you should believe in yourself too.

But back to the story of the eagle, it all changed when you read the last sentence. That's when the history of the eagle changed from being a chicken to a true eagle – he lifted his wings, **he ACTED**. He did something. After he knew he was an eagle, he acted, with help.

This book has been your help. Don't think for a minute it was a coincidence that you stumbled upon it or read it based on a recommendation – no! God ordained it before you were born, HE ordained it. The question is this: Now that you know the treasures you carry, now that you know what God has deposited in you, now that you know God has made you an answer to the groaning and cries of all creation—are you just going to sit there and not ACT? No, I don't want you to see it as though if you don't act you have only disappointed yourself, no, not at all. The truth is this, if you don't act, if you don't become God's answer to creation, you will be forcing people to believe God does not exist. Oh hold on! Better still, you would be keeping the whole of creation in groaning and pain until you manifest the glory of the diamonds God has placed in you.

Listen to me. I am not asking you to act simply because you have to. You must come to the point of understanding that by God's own sovereign move there are *several* destinies and dreams hanging onto yours. Yes, that's right. If you don't shine your light, others won't. It's just how phenomenally important the manifestation of your destiny is. Your family, your children, people you don't know, generations yet unborn, thousands and millions – it's all hanging on your neck. Now, you think it's just okay to know about your talents and abilities and strengths and just sit on it? Try again.

It's pretty much like the comparison I made earlier in this book about being your country's ambassador to another country. Say you are a citizen of country "A" and you've been sent down to country "B" as an ambassador. Your government from country A has provided you with **everything** you'll need to function properly as an ambassador in country B – an excellently staffed office with the best minds in every possible industry who even accurately know what will happen in the future (Holy Spirit), a beautiful and comfortable house that never runs out of food and all the necessary amenities to make your life comfortable (God's providence), full armoured security service that protects you 24/7 (angels on assignment), all the resources you'll need to act in the interest of the government of country A (people God has connected you to), a very detailed full-proof manual to guide you in every single action as an ambassador (the Bible), and even all the skills, experiences, and abilities needed to succeed outstandingly (God's diamond in you), a telephone system that connects you directly to the bedside phone of the president of your country A (prayer), etc.

Now, imagine you have all these at your disposal, and all you do day in day out is sit under a shady tree in front of your house in your shorts and sunglasses and watch passers by on foot and in their cars and dogs running past or chasing cats. Hey! WAKE UP! You are an ambassador with credentials. When the president of A sent you over to country B, he had a little chat with the president of country B and this is what he said: "I am sending down my finest to represent me in your country. (S)he's the best I've got and whatever (s)he does or says is an exact reflection of me, so take him (her) very serious."

Please tell me, honestly, how you would feel if you were the president of country A. Tell me how you would really feel if you were told that your ambassador just sits under a tree all day and watches passers by, and people in country B are beginning to think country A is actually useless and good for nothing? Be honest now. Tell me how you would feel knowing that with all that provision you made for your ambassador, he hasn't acted in any way that reflects you as a very powerful president.

Right! Now let's get biblical shall we? In Luke 9:59-62 (AMP) we read about this interesting encounter:

> *"And He (Jesus) said to another, Become My disciple, side with my party, and accompany Me! But he replied, Lord, permit me first to go and bury (await the death of) my father. But Jesus said to him, allow the dead to bury their own dead; but as for you, go and publish abroad throughout all regions the kingdom of God. Another also said, I will follow You, Lord, and become Your disciple and side with Your party; but let me first say good-bye to those at my home. Jesus said to him, No one who puts his hand to the plough and looks back [to the things behind] is fit for the kingdom of God."*

The core insight of this encounter was Jesus' attempt to make known one and only one thing – when you hear His voice or His command (in whatever form it comes), ACT on it immediately; not later, immediately. Don't forget the Messiah Jesus was a Jew. He thoroughly understood the Torah. He knew that the entire problem of Israel not reaching the Promised Land in time after they left Egypt was as a result of one problem – they didn't ACT on God's direction when they heard it.

Now this should get you thinking. Israel was meant to reach Canaan in approximately eleven to fourteen days walking (according to historians). It took them forty years instead. You should be asking yourself – if you refuse to ACT on the direction of God (irrespective of the form it comes in), are you ready to wander in life's wilderness for another forty years? If it happened to a whole nation (a nation God declared to be His own beloved one), then it shouldn't be too hard happening to you – think about it.

Anyway, back to the point in question. When Jesus said to the young man, *"allow the dead to go bury their own dead,"* the young man had no clue what it meant. Jesus came to the young man so that he may have life and have it more abundantly (John 10:10) only if he was smart enough to accept the Saviour at that point in time. Jesus was trying to tell the young man "the person you are going to bury is dead because they didn't hearken and ACT just like you are attempting to do now, therefore if you go back, you would be associating yourself to the same death by procrastination that your father experienced." It was not necessarily a physical death but a figurative expression of the fact that the young man's father was no more "***in the present time***" just in the same way that dead people cannot experience "***the now.***" Dead people cannot take advantage of the opportunities that "***the now***" presents; they cannot have a first chance if that was the only one available. In other words, the young man was being asked by Jesus to consider his decision of transporting himself from "***the now***" to the "***no more available now***" – it was a matter of choice, and which of these times he chose to be in was dependent on whether he (the young man) ACTED now or later.

If he acted now, he would be present in "***the now***" timeframe and every opportunity it brought with it. If he chose later, "***the now***" time would have been gone and so also the opportunities that came with it. The great apostle Paul understood this concept so precisely when he reiterated in 2 Corinthians 6:1-2, *"We then, as workers together with Him also plead with you not to receive the grace of God in vain. For He says: 'In an **acceptable time** I have heard you, and in the day of salvation I have helped you.' **Behold, now is the accepted time; behold, now is the day of salvation**"*—not tomorrow, not later, but now. ACT now.

I don't know of another way to emphasize the importance of ACTING now. God is not an idle God; neither is His Son Jesus Christ nor His Holy Spirit. God is a God of perfection, and He is timely in the least. Seriously, if God is speaking all these things to you right now, through me as a vessel and this book as a medium, do you really think He doesn't need you to act on them now? Do you honestly think He is telling you these things at this very moment because He only needs you to act on them in two weeks' time or in two years' time? Do you really think God has that kind of time? Don't you think God could have also just waited until this year to allow the nation of Israel to enter Canaan? After all a thousand years is like a day unto the Lord right? Or perhaps He could have just been lackadaisical and waited till the year 2036 to bring about salvation.

God means business when He speaks. When He tells you (as He is doing now), it is because He is ready to ACT with you. I am sorry, if He is ready and you are not, He's not going to hang around for you. Hello? Who is the greater of the two? You or Him? So how come you want Him to wait for you until you are ready? Who created who? Now, the last bit of the scripture from Luke 9 above says, *"No one who puts his hand to the plough and looks back [to the things behind] is fit for the kingdom of God."*

See, when you enter into an employment, you first go through an interview process. This process is merely to determine whether you are fit for the job. I said fit for the job. If the main success factor of the organisation is "TRUST" for example (maybe it's a legal firm) then alongside everything else "trust" is one of the main areas of fitness you will be tested on. Just like in the army, endurance is one of the main fitness areas you will be tested on. I am an accountant, and I am certain one main area of fitness I would be tested on if I were looking for a role in financial management would be "integrity."

God's kingdom is also an organisation in itself. You think He will just lump everybody in? God is the CEO (chief executive officer) in His organisation, the remunerations are far more than excellent, and the working conditions are amazingly indescribable, but one of the main areas of fitness you will be tested on in order to join in is *whether you can do what the CEO tells you to do.*

Can you ACT on what God tells you to do, when He tells you to do it, and how He tells you to do it? Well if you can't then you are purely not fit for the Organisation, and if you are not fit, why in the name of heaven are you still expecting the CEO to pay you all the remunerations and benefits?

Come, let's reason together. Let's face facts—even in a secular company, if the CEO had a strategic vision for the company and gave some directions to be followed by each employee, your decision to show any form of disobedience towards the CEO's directions would most likely result in the entire organisation going into a demise. Now if you were the CEO, how long would you tolerate an employee who didn't want to act on the direction you gave him/her knowing very well that the entire organisation is wired like a clockwork and if one part messes up, the whole organisation gets messed up? Can you afford it?

Hebrews 3:7-10 says:

> "Therefore, as the Holy Spirit says: 'Today, if you will hear His voice, **Do not harden your hearts as in the rebellion**, in the day of trial in the wilderness, where your fathers tested Me, tried Me, and saw My works forty years. Therefore I was angry with that generation, and said, "They always go astray in their heart, and they have not known My ways."'"

The phrase "Do not harden your heart" suggests that ("**do**") whether your heart gets hardened after you hear the voice of God is a matter of choice – YOU choose whether to do what God is suggesting to you. In fact it means you have the power to do or not to do. Now that changes the whole dynamics of what excuse you can give yourself and God for not acting immediately after reading this book. You can no more say "the seed was planted in you and the devil came to snatch it away," neither can you say "I didn't act because I was waiting to put x, y, and z into place first."

This time round it's a choice you are going to make. In the case of Pharaoh of Egypt, God Himself hardened his heart but imagine the wrath Pharaoh got in return – think about the scenario where YOU deliberately choose to harden your heart. Act now. It's good for your own destiny and that of those around you.

Act now, put some works to your faith, and do something. God is ready to act with you so please act. Don't lose all the opportunities that have arrived with this "*now*" time. There is a reason why God chose "*this time*" and not tomorrow. Act now;

you'll be glad you did. Not very many get a second chance; trust me, if there were so many chances, you would have read again about the young man who went to bury his father first or the other who went to say goodbye to the people of his house – you would have read about them in the Bible coming back from the burial and goodbye trip to still meet Jesus waiting for them. The sad truth is that when they were ready, Jesus was somewhere else and so was every opportunity He made available to those two young men when they met Him the first time.

You need to make a choice and it's quite simple. You can act now or act later; you can journey for fourteen days or struggle for the next forty years; God won't feel bad about it. He gave you a perfect opportunity. All you had to say, and I hope you do say it, is this – "If you are ready to act O LORD, then I am acting now also."

I want to end this chapter with a somewhat interesting story. I want to believe you who are reading this book would agree with me that the phenomenal importance of the telephone in our world today would make its inventor by far the richest man in the world a hundred times over. Think about it. Google, Facebook, the Internet, all depend on what started off as the telephone. If you can't imagine that, then imagine the number of homes and offices in the world that use a "telephone." It's therefore not hard at all to imagine that whoever invented the telephone, if they were alive currently, would easily be the richest man in the world, and like I said, several times over. Now read on.

Well, there are two persons in this story—one of them goes by the name Alexander Graham Bell, known the world over and in history as the man who invented the telephone. The other man I want to introduce to you is Elisha Gray. Well, Elisha was born on August 2, 1835, into a Quaker family somewhere on a farm in Barnesville, Ohio. He spent some of his years at Oberlin College experimenting with electrical devices and later ended up in Chicago as an electrician.

To cut a long story short, Elisha Gray had invented a telephone that used a liquid microphone, and he had asked his lawyer to file an application for a "provisional patent" (also called a caveat patent) for his invention on the Monday morning of February 14, 1876. A few hours later on that same morning, Alexander Graham Bell's lawyers had come in to file for a "full patent" for a similar invention on his behalf (but not quite as powerful as that of Elisha Gray's telephone). But it was for a full patent. On arriving at the patents office, Alexander and his lawyers got to know that Elisha Gray had just put in a provisional patent for a telephone with a liquid component. They without hesitation **ACTED**. They quickly included an insert on their full patent application to say that Alexander's telephone also involved a liquid component. Considering that Alexander filed a full application first as opposed to Gray's provisional application, Alexander's patent was considered the "first to invent," thus denying Gray of his one time opportunity of raking in all the immeasurable benefits of being the first to invent the telephone.

Irrespective of the slightly dubious nature of Alexander's action, the fact still remains that Elisha had the invention first, he got to the patents office first, and he had the opportunity to file a full application first, but that's not the fact I want to emphasize here. Mr. Elisha Gray had every opportunity to be the inventor of the telephone (in fact he was) but **he did NOT ACT**. It's that simple. He did not ACT. So for his prize, he was not the one who turned out to plough all that wealth, he was not the one to go down in history as one of the greatest inventors, he was not the one to bask in the fame, he was not the one to whom statues were erected in honour – it was Alexander Graham Bell. He acted. He acted. He acted.

I must congratulate you for reading this book up until this point. It only means you have put your hands to the plough. You'll never know the exceeding goodness, the flowing milk, and the sweet honey that await you beyond this point until you act. It will start from when you finish reading the last line of this book. But let me remind you about something we both know – God does not only speak to us through dreams, prophecies, and the Bible. Not at all; if we think that way, then we are putting a limitation on God's expansive sovereignty. God can and will speak to us through anything He wishes – even donkeys. Today it has pleased the LORD Almighty to use this book as a medium of speaking to you.

I am a practicing accountant; I did not just get up one day and decide "Okay! Now I am going to write a book for my fellow

Christians." Uh-uh! I was led by the Holy Spirit every step of the way. In fact I have probably learnt more from this book than anyone else may have. It was a medium God used to teach me the very things it may be teaching you also. In fact if anyone had told me a day or two before I started writing this book, I most likely would have told them "you are the greatest joker on earth below and in heaven above." But, alas, when the Spirit of God arrested my mind and troubled my soul day and night, I had to take notice and walk in obedience.

In 2 Timothy 3:16 the Bible says:

"All Scripture is given by inspiration of God, and is profitable for doctrine, for reproof, for correction, for instruction in righteousness."

Do not be confused in thinking "scripture" is only limited to the "Bible." If you do, the tendency then would be that even when God is using non-Bible means to minister to you directions which will be profitable for your doctrine, reproof, correction, and instructions in righteousness, you might reject them simply because they are not written in the Bible or because they were not written by Moses, or Paul, or Peter, or John.

Did God's inspiration or God's ability to speak to us through men come to an end with the going to sleep of Moses, or Paul, or Peter, or John? Certainly not; in fact the word *scripture* comes from the Latin word *scriptura*, which simply means "writings."

The text in 2 Timothy 3:16 can thus be rewritten as this: *"All writing which is given by inspiration of God, is profitable for doctrine, for reproof, for correction, for instruction in righteousness."* What differentiates these writings from any other ordinary writing you will find in newspapers and in a Harry Porter book for example is that our writings are inspired by the Spirit of the Most High God.

It's been a marvellous journey for me, and I trust that it has been for you also. Whatever this book will achieve, I publicly declare that it be all lifted to the great Hashem, the God of Israel, as a sweet-smelling offering of praise. Indeed I am grateful to God for leading you to read it – believe me when I say to you it is NOT a coincidence or luck that you read this book.

My last insight: The Hebrew language is the original language with which God communicated with man. I like to think of it as the holy language. Personally, if God chose it as good enough for Him, then it sure as heaven is more than good enough for me also. Every single aspect of the Hebrew language, from the way the letters are drawn up through to the number assignable to each of them and right down to how words are composed by joining these letters, is an intentional creation by God Himself. Now, the fascinating thing I want to bring to your attention is this – in the Hebrew language there is no word *luck*, neither is there a word for "coincidence" or "chance." The absence of these words is in themselves God trying to convey a message to us – there is no such thing as luck or coincidence. God is that meticulous, and nothing works outside His enclosure. So what am I saying? That your reading this book was already planned out before you were born; it didn't just happen, so I'd recommend you don't take it lightly. It's easy to try and rationalize by saying "oh, I saw the book in an advertisement" or "a friend recommended it," but hey! Hold on! There are millions who saw the ad but never read the book, so why you? There will also have been millions who read it but never told their friends or family about it, so why you and why now?

It is my prayer that God Himself, by His mighty right hand, will guide you to discover the hectares and hectares of diamonds and treasures He Himself has deposited in you as the Bible says in 2 Corinthians 4:7: ***"But we have this treasure in earthen vessels, that the excellence of the power may be of God and not of us."*** I pray earnestly that God will open your eyes to see the exceeding goodness that resides in you. You have the very breath of God in you, the same breath by which He spoke the earth into being.

I say this one thing to you – God is not a man that He should lie; if He says take a step then take a step. You are the Eden in which God's diamonds of Glory have been deposited. Bring it forth and let the Glory of God be made manifest……. There are diamonds in you – bring them out. SHALOM!

PRAYER POINTS:

1. Pray, THANKING GOD for His goodness towards you in reading this book and for His great glory that is about to be revealed from inside of you.

AUTHOR'S OTHER WORKS

Title:	Is This Why Africa Is? (E-book & Paperback)
Description:	I ask all the questions about Africa that nobody else will. Deep, profound questions
Availability:	Amazon & Kindle
Link to View:	http://goo.gl/ecRMig

Title:	Where Did God Hide His Diamonds? (E-book & Paperback)
Description:	Discovering what exactly God has hidden in you, finding it & prospering freely from it
Availability:	Amazon & Kindle
Link to View:	http://goo.gl/ecRMig

Title:	Doing Business with God (E-book & Paperback)
Description:	60 shocking biblical principles for extraordinary leadership, business and politics.
Availability:	Amazon & Kindle
Link to View:	http://goo.gl/ecRMig

Title:	Midnight Philosophies (E-book & Paperback)
Description:	My Deep thoughts, Philosophies, Reflections – Whispers of my mind.
Availability:	Amazon & Kindle
Link to View:	http://goo.gl/ecRMig

Title:	This Godly Child of Mine (E-book & Paperback)
Description:	A revelatory book on how to raise godly children in a perverse and lawless world
Availability:	Amazon & Kindle
Link to View:	http://goo.gl/ecRMig

Title:	The Deputy Minister for Corruption (E-book & Paperback)
Description:	A Novel
Availability:	Amazon & Kindle
Link to View:	http://goo.gl/ecRMig

Title:	A Dove in the Storm (E-book & Paperback)
Description:	A Novel
Availability:	Amazon & Kindle
Link to View:	http://goo.gl/ecRMig

Title:	100% JOB INTERVIEW SUCCESS (E-book & Paperback)
Description:	A simple, straightforward guide to passing every job interview you attend.
Availability:	Amazon & Kindle
Link to View:	http://goo.gl/ecRMig

Title:	Bible-by-Heart (Mobile App)
Description:	A simple but effective App to help anyone memorize 500 Bible verses in a year.

Availability:	iTunes & Google Play Stores
Link to View:	http://goo.gl/T3UdPN (i-Tunes)
Link to View:	http://goo.gl/ljnECR (Android)

Title:	Holy Rat (Mobile Game)
Description:	An exciting Christian mobile game that unwittingly gets you addicted to the word.
Availability:	iTunes & Google Play Stores
Link to View:	http://goo.gl/bygjBi (i-Tunes)
Link to View:	http://goo.gl/F18RM0 (Android)

ABOUT THE AUTHOR

Marricke Kofi Gane, is a gifted African Author, Philosopher, Public Speaker, Coach and Educationist. His writings carry real depth, are highly motivating yet challenging every status quo. He displays dexterity of mind and refined humour where appropriate. He is never shy in some of his works, to show a strong balance between his Christian roots and the reality of living in today's world.

Discover for yourself, all that his writings stand for - to dare, to motivate, to impact!! For more on him, visit www.marrickekofigane.com

Dear Reader,

Thank you for reading this book. I am hopeful that the information provided in it has given you some new learning, challenged you, or provided some answers and inspiration.

I respectfully ask your indulgence in 2 simple ways:

1. Whatever positive action(s) this book has inspired you to take, DO IT NOW. Not later.

2. Help other potential readers who without you, may never read this book by simply following the link below to leave a review. It only takes 3 minutes, but it could be a lifetime blessing for someone out there.

   http://goo.gl/v03bu2

Thank you once again for everything

Marricke Kofi GANE

www.ingramcontent.com/pod-product-compliance
Lightning Source LLC
Chambersburg PA
CBHW061325040426
42444CB00011B/2775